# LATIN BY
# STAVE ANALYSIS

A LINGUISTIC APPROACH TO GRAMMAR AND TRANSLATION

*by*

HARRY SCHOFIELD, M.A. (CANTAB), M.ED.

Principal Lecturer in Education
Bognor College of Education

D1822867

9780852254905

EDUCATIONAL EXPLORERS LIMITED
READING · BERKSHIRE · ENGLAND

*First published in Great Britain 1969*
*by Educational Explorers Ltd*
*40 Silver Street, Reading, RG1 2SU*
© H. Schofield 1969
SBN: 85225 490 3

*Printed in Great Britain*
*by Lamport Gilbert Printers Ltd*
*Reading, Berkshire*
*Set in Monotype Imprint*

# CONTENTS

# APPENDICES

## ACKNOWLEDGEMENTS

We are grateful to the following authors and publishers for their permission to reproduce the passages in the text:

Charles C. Fries's LINGUISTICS AND READING
Holt, Rinehart & Winston, Inc.,

Robert Lado LANGUAGES TEACHING: A SCIENTIFIC APPROACH
McGraw-Hill Book Company

William Haas's LINGUISTIC RELEVANCE
Longmans Green & Company

# FOREWORD

When I received Mr Schofield's typescript I knew at once that he had something to offer which would help all learners and teachers of the Latin language. Hence at once I was prepared to welcome his text among those we publish in our Language Series. This text is the original work submitted to me by Mr Schofield.

Meeting with the author and talking about our work, it seemed to both of us that our ideas could add to each other's view of the field and we agreed to explore together the possibilities of merging our techniques in the production of a complete Latin course. This we are involved in organising now, but in order not to deprive Latin teachers of such a fine idea as stave analysis we do not delay publication of the text that presents it as it was before our meeting.

It will be clear to many that all inflected languages can profit from stave analysis. Since we have become aware of this, our language team has been at work and we hope to publish in the near future helpful material capable of accelerating learning in those languages as we have accelerated it in some non-inflected ones.

Caleb Gattegno
*General Editor*

*Chapter One*

## INTRODUCTION

THE AIM OF THIS TEXT is to present a new method of translating from Latin into English. It is a method that can be applied to simple four word sentences in the first year of the Latin course and, by logical development, to the long, difficult sentences encountered in the later years, when the learner meets, in unsimplified form, the writings of Livy, Caesar and Cicero with all their linguistic complexities. The method is *stave analysis*[1] and is based on two important linguistic features: the marker (especially that indicating dependence, as well as the inflection marker) and the hierarchical structure of complex sentences. Earlier chapters will deal with the problems that made the development of this new method necessary, and will show how it is applied in the initial stages of Latin teaching. Chapter Four will show how it is applied to complex sentences.

C. C. Fries[2] emphasises that, although momentous advances have been made in the science of linguistics, cultural lag frequently prevents these findings from being incorporated into more scientific teaching methods. This is true in the field of Latin teaching. Research is constantly being conducted into better methods of teaching science, mathematics and modern languages, yet teachers of Latin are still debating whether a modified form of the old grammar-translation method—the ancestors of which are a belief in Mental Faculties and Formal Discipline—is less effective than the Direct Method, which began with Quintilian and was revived by the schoolmasters of the Renaissance when Latin was still a spoken language. In terms of linguistic findings such debate resembles a discussion about the comparative merits and effectiveness of the gas and

[1]From an original idea of Dr. E. A. Lunzer.
[2]*The Structure of English*, Introduction, p. 1.

9

paraffin lamps, both of which have been rendered obsolete by the advent of electric light.

Although current methods of teaching Latin grammar frequently entail rote learning, as in the disciplinary approach, they generally have a rationale that is easily recognised and explained (though not so easily justified). There is, also, generally a fair degree of standardisation of method within any one school of thought: rarely is the method entirely haphazard. Yet investigation has shown that many teachers, when asked what method they use for teaching translation, either fail to explain any clearly discernible method, or admit that they do not use any one method alone, especially when translating complex sentences. In the early stages of simple Latin, grammar and translation advance side by side; later there seems to be a widening gap between the two and an unsystematic approach to the whole problem of translation. That there are many excellent teachers of Latin is not for a moment denied; but there are too many with insufficiently modern and precise ideas about the teaching of their subject.

One frequently hears the complaint that there is no suitable reading book for pupils at about the third year of a four year Latin course to 'O' level.[1] A course book of structured Latin to coincide with the learning of precise grammatical points is used for the first two years; but this, say the teachers, leaves an unbridgeable gap between this structured Latin and that of Roman authors.

Such an admission is tragic and a serious indictment of the methods used to teach translation in the first two years. This text will show that the fault lies in teachers' being unduly concerned with rendering Latin sentences in terms of English words or equivalent meaning, and insufficiently concerned with the fundamental structure of the Latin sentence. The complaint that there is no suitable reading material at a given point in the course implies that there is some essential difference between simple and complex sentences in Latin, making them entirely distinct linguistic phenomena. Such a claim is patently untrue; and, because it is untrue, there is no justification for using

[1]General Certificate of Education, Ordinary Level.

different methods to teach translation of simple and complex sentences.

The method many use for teaching translation of simple Latin sentences breaks down when applied to complex sentences. This text will show that this frequently occurs because teachers are concerning themselves with the item, or word, rather than with the structure of the total sentence.

A danger of opinions is that they may become accepted as fact and there are methods of teaching based on opinions as though on facts. These include methods of teaching Latin, many of which are even founded on misconceptions. This may come as a surprise to teachers who have never analysed the opinions underlying the method they are using, to determine whether these have real substance; they have heard opinions expressed so often that they have come to accept them without question.

The writer's research began with an examination of several such misconceptions. One held that the difficulty in translating from Latin into English lay in the order of words peculiar to Latin. That this cannot be entirely the case is easily shown by the number of simple sentences first year students of Latin translate correctly without difficulty. In almost any language one may encounter a non-English word order, but it is not suggested that this makes the learning of, for example, German unusually difficult. Indeed, pointing out to students such differences of word order or, more correctly, of speech pattern is a comparatively simple exercise in contrastive linguistics (see Chapter Two).

One has only to put the words of a Latin sentence in an English order to disprove the claim that the Latin word order causes the serious translation errors or the failure to make any sense out of a given passage. For when

Marcus amicum suum Romae videt

Marcus sees his friend in Rome

was altered to

Marcus videt suum amicum Romae

it was found that no improvement in translation accuracy resulted. When the word order was altered in the longer and more complex sentences met at fourth and fifth form level, translation sense still broke down—sometimes in part, sometimes entirely. The word-order belief was clearly an example of a misconception that had become accepted as a fact. Even if it could be shown that simplifying the word order did help some students to some extent, by what linguistic criteria would the pupil, in the absence of help from the teacher, alter the word order for himself prior to translating?

Another view commonly held and easily shown to be lacking in substance is that error in translating into English is caused by vocabulary. That is to say that, if pupils only knew the meaning of every single Latin word in a text, they would be able to produce a correct translation. To test this hypothesis the writer gave Latin passages to eight hundred pupils of fourth and fifth form level (age 15 and 16) and supplied all the meanings in English of the Latin words. The marks obtained for the passages ranged from 7 to 97 per cent. These results suggested that this was another case of a misconception masquerading as a fact.

Naturally, if we do not know the meaning of any words in a language, we cannot begin to translate that language into English. But in the early stages of language learning, especially by the grammar/translation method, lists of Latin words with their English equivalents are learnt by rote before translation begins. Consequently it is highly unlikely that the 'vocabulary' theory obtains in the early stages of the Latin course. Again, the more Latin the student encounters as he makes progress through the course, the smaller the proportion of unknown to known words. Looked at from any angle, and principally from that of large scale experiment, the vocabulary error factor is clearly a misconception accepted as fact through lack of examination.

From the foregoing observation the need obviously exists for a new approach to Latin teaching—and especially to the teaching of translation into English—based on objective findings rather than on preconceptions.

Stave analysis, which is proposed as the means to fill this void, does not, however, hold better, or more accurate, translation as a sufficient end in itself. This method is a means of teaching the learner ultimately to read Latin. For stave analysis reflects the mental behaviour and processes which the skilled reader of Latin employs automatically and in the early stages of using the method presents this behaviour in visual form. This will be treated more fully later in the text.

The problem of reading introduces yet another misconception in the minds of some teachers. Here we are concerned with those who teach by the Direct Method. In *The Teaching of Classics*[1] it is claimed that this method dispenses with formal translation in order to allow 'wider reading of Latin authors'. Elsewhere in the same work it is suggested that translation be taught at a later stage as 'an art in itself'. There may well be a great difference in artistic content between, for example, a Furneaux translation of Tacitus and the average schoolboy's rendering of passages by the same writer. Yet it is very difficult to see how Latin can be read before one is able to translate—unless reading is taken to mean the production of sounds for the written symbols, a similar activity to that of the young child in the primary school first learning to read aloud. This interpretation of reading explains why parents are surprised when their child, skilful at the calculation required in mechanical arithmetic, is unable to cope with problems in arithmetic. They are even more surprised when told that the fault lies in their child's inability to read: they know that their child is good at reading—provided this is interpreted as good at producing sounds for written symbols as distinct from deriving meaning from the various combinations of symbols. This point is well emphasised by Gates:[2]

> Reading is not a simple mechanical skill; nor is it a narrow scholastic tool. Properly cultivated, it is essentially a thoughtful process . . . It should be developed as a complex organisation of higher mental processes. It can, and should, embrace all types of thinking, evaluating, judging, imagining, reasoning and problem solving.

and later:

> . . . a definition of reading limited to desirable habits of recognition and comprehension is inadequate to meet current needs.

[1]See bibliography.
[2]Cited apud Fries, *Linguistics and Reading*, p. 117.

Lado[1] warns that there are dangers in the underlying assumptions of the direct method. These are rarely appreciated by those who advocate its use.

The direct method assumes that learning a foreign language is the same as learning the mother tongue; that is, by exposing the student directly to the foreign language, it impresses itself perfectly on the mind. This is true only up to a point, since the psychology of second language learning differs from that of learning a first. A child is forced to learn the first language because he has no other way to express his wants. In a second language this is largely missing, since the student knows that he can communicate through his native tongue when necessary. Furthermore, with the first language the child's mind can be thought of as a tabula rasa where patterns become impressed, whereas with the second language the habits of the first language are already there, and the second language is perceived through the habit channels of the native tongue.

and

The direct method overcame two major faults of the grammar-translation method by substituting language contact for grammar recitation, and language use for translation.[2]

The advocates of the direct method, failing to achieve results for a variety of reasons, drifted in the 1930's into the more limited goal of 'reading knowledge'. This was a purely passive understanding of graded readings with dictionary help on difficult words.

The need for persons who could speak foreign languages during the second world war showed the inadequacy of this 'reading knowledge' as a first step towards efficient reading . . . Reading itself tended to remain inefficient because it did not operate through full control of language.

[1] *Language Teaching ; A Scientific Approach*, Introduction, pp. 5–6.
[2] This refers to the use of the direct method to teach modern (spoken) languages. The case for Latin is rather different.

Finally, Fries[1] has this to say about the process of learning to read:

> In the basic analysis of the nature of the reading process itself and of the precise task of learning to read, we must defer consideration of the use to which reading may be put as well as the abilities which may be developed through reading. To learn to walk, a child must first achieve such muscular co-ordination as will enable him to keep his upright balance by pushing with his feet on something solid . . . All consideration of the uses of the skill of walking must be postponed until the first stages of the learning process have been mastered. For these first stages it is necessary to discover exactly what must be learnt.

Stave analysis aims to 'provide something solid on which the learner can press to keep his upright balance'. Because it shows at the visual level and the conscious level exactly those processes which the mind of the reader performs automatically and unconsciously—as with any perfected skill—it is thought to represent exactly what must be learnt. Only if translation can avoid the criticism of being an end in itself and a formal exercise, because it is the 'learning to stand' followed by reading which is the 'learning to walk', can it be justified and systematically taught. There is no short-cut to a full mastery of reading: and the claim that pupils, by avoiding formal translation, will be able to read a wider range of authors could come dangerously close to attempting to avoid the process of learning to stand. Reading can only operate through full control of the language, and such full control can in turn only operate through a full knowledge of structure. It is this that stave analysis is designed to give.

This matter of structure is crucially important. The greatest single advance in linguistics came, according to Fries, when the school of linguistics now known as structuralists asserted that attention must be transferred from the item, or word, to the *structure*. This brings us back to our contention that to attempt to simplify translation by simplifying *word* order is misconceived; the simplification of word order not only lays emphasis

[1]*Linguistics and Reading*, p. 118.

on the item or word instead of on the structure, but also, in certain circumstances, altering the word order may damage the structure. Meaning is on the one hand lexical meaning of the individual words and on the other the functional meaning of these items operating in structures. Within a given structure a word takes on functional meaning in relation to other words. The first step in ascertaining meaning is not to seek the lexical equivalent meanings in English of the Latin words but to determine the parameters within which certain words operate.

Even well-intentioned advice can produce the wrong emphasis. Not infrequently the learner of Latin is urged to look at the word-ending, and later in this text we shall look at the word-ending but in a structural context. The conventional form of this advice draws attention again to the particular word or item, when attention should be drawn to the relation of the word to other words. In fact the accusative ending *um* of a Latin word *dominum* tells us no more about a person known in Latin as *dominus*, and in English as a slave-master, than does the nominative ending *us*; but the two endings denote very different functions of the word in relation to other words. The ending indicates the role the person plays. The English meaning of *dominus* is irrelevant until the function of this item and its relationship to the other items in the Latin structure have been determined. It is possible to substitute *feminam* for *dominum*: the word fulfils the same structural function although the lexical meaning is different; or to substitute *domini*, in which case the functional meaning is different and the lexical meaning the same. In either instance the lexical meaning is of secondary importance for the beginner.

Evidence that this emphasis is lacking in much Latin teaching is found in pupils' turning to the dictionary at once on being asked to translate a piece of Latin into English. From their speed in doing this one observes that they do not stop to consider structures and parameters, and one can deduce that they are concerned with the lexical meaning of the first word they do not know in the text. Yet even if the meaning of the word is unknown to them, the ending, or *inflection marker*, reveals the precise role and function of the word, the appreciation of which is a prerequisite of correct translation.

16

Further evidence of incorrect emphasis in the teaching of translation techniques is available in the excessive to-and-fro eye movement of pupils embarking on a translation. The eye movement is frequently accompanied by finger movement over the printed page, and by lip movement. The erratic eye movement is indicative of emphasis on items rather than on structure, and it might be possible to establish that the quality of the final translation is inversely related to the amount of such eye movement. Fries[1] observes that excessive to-and-fro eye movement in a child reading his mother tongue is symptomatic of defective reading ability and not the cause of poor reading performance. Such movement with Latin suggests that the translator is not making responses to the words in the passage in the order in which they appear, and that his eye, and consequently his mind also, finds it necessary to return frequently to words to which a correct response should already have been made. In addition it suggests that the child is attempting to build up his structures item by item, abstracting these items one by one from different parts of the Latin sentence.

R. L. Politzer[2] states that, while on some occasions French builds the bridge of communication stone by stone—the stones being what we have described above as items—in precisely the same order as does English, there are many occasions when the languages use different speech patterns to convey the same information or idea. In such cases the learner must make himself familiar with the patterns rather than with the individual items that make up the pattern. Politzer states further that in comprehension it is the *structure* of the pattern which must be learnt, while in production emphasis must be on the pattern content.

For example, no pupil should find it too hard to translate:
    mon ami est intelligent
as
    my friend is intelligent;
nor should it be impossibly difficult for him to appreciate that
    il faut qu'il soit sage

[1]*Linguistics and Reading*, pp. 23 and 31.
[2]*Teaching French; An Introduction to Applied Linguistics* (See bibliography).

and
> he must behave himself

convey the same idea, although the speech patterns in the two languages are dissimilar.

In Latin the learner has to make a minor adjustment even in the case of the first sentence, which would appear as:
> meus amicus sapiens est

or equally as
> amicus meus sapiens est.

Were we to produce the same item order, or the same order of stones to build the bridge of communication as that used in both French and English, we should obtain:
> meus amicus est sapiens;

this, however, now emphasises the quality of intelligence in a way not to be found in either the English or the French sentences.

Later the pupil will be required to learn that
> he comes to see

is represented in Latin by
> venit ut videat

and hardly ever, except very occasionally in verse, by
> venit videre.

But, if such a simple problem is the real reason why twelve-year-old pupils beginning to learn Latin find the language difficult, there could be little hope of children ever learning their mother tongue, which presents much greater problems and at an age when their linguistic experience is far more limited. Furthermore it is only the brightest of the grammar school children who are confronted with such a problem, while bright and dull alike face the complexities of the mother tongue.

Many teachers using the direct method appreciate the main point that Politzer makes above, but it is doubtful if many distinguish as clearly as he does—and the distinction is vital—between the arts of comprehension and production, and the subtly different pattern emphasis required for each. Consequently their method of dealing with the problem is inadequate.

Noam Chomsky[1] makes a distinction similar to Politzer's when talking of children acquiring the mother tongue. He says that a distinction must be made between the receptive control

[1] *The Acquisition of Language*, pp. 40–41.

of grammar (comprehension) and productive control of grammar (speech). Chomsky further states that the diary study of child speech and its development shows that comprehension is in advance of production, and that the same thing can be said of second language learning. Thus the production which receives such emphasis by the exponents of the direct method, and which is a synthesis, requires analysis of structure if it is to result in full command of the language, especially of a language which is no longer spoken. This analytical emphasis is frequently lacking in direct method teaching.

The aim of the present work is to incorporate the discoveries of modern linguistics in a Latin teaching method, one that is not only more systematic and more effective for translating complex Latin but more effective in teaching Latin ab initio.

This text concentrates on translation since this was the pressing problem tackled first. But it must not be thought, from what has been already said, that no importance is attached to problems posed by 'vocabulary' or 'lexical meaning'. However, the writer's investigations have shown that these are far from being the main problems posed by translation from Latin into English, and that emphasis placed on them—like the slogans and rules of thumb which are often the basis for a teaching method—only serves to draw attention away from the fundamental problems.

Finally, there are teachers of Latin who spend countless hours in debate on points which, while certainly important, are far from fundamental and cannot make any just claim on time which could with much greater profit be devoted to more pressing problems. Such points are: modifications of the content of the syllabus for certain public examinations, with little regard for methods of increasing ability of the candidates to deal with what content there is; whether prose composition has a right to be included at certain stages of the syllabus or whether it ought to be excluded entirely; how to make Latin more interesting and attractive and hence help to halt the drift away from Latin studies.

No teacher of any subject will deny the importance of interest if successful learning is to take place. But what is the difference between an interesting and a dull textbook if the pupil's linguistic ability is so limited that he cannot derive meaning from either? One of the greatest stimuli to interest is success and mastery of a new subject. Such mastery will be far more effective than all attempts to produce artificial interest without an improvement in teaching method resulting in greater mastery of the Latin language.

*Chapter Two*

# THE REAL MEANING OF WORD ORDER

IN THE PREVIOUS CHAPTER it was suggested that many misconceptions exist about the nature and significance of the word order peculiar to Latin. In particular the argument that translating Latin is difficult because the Latin and English word orders to convey the same idea differ was held to be untenable. We advanced the view that it is a comparatively simple lesson in contrastive linguistics to show the beginner that where English says:

Marcus sees Sextus

using the order 1 2 3, Latin, to express the same idea, says:

**Marcus Sextum** vid**et**

using the order 1 3 2.

If English alters the order of the words and says:

Sextus sees Marcus

the meaning of the sentence changes: we have a new situation and a new idea expressed with Sextus and Marcus changing roles. This change is produced by transposing the representative words in the English sentence. Latin on the other hand can say:

**Marcus Sextum** vid**et**

**Sextum Marcus** vid**et**

vid**et Sextum Marcus**

without altering the original idea that Marcus sees Sextus. Countless teachers have made this elementary point very early in the Latin course. In a non-inflected language the functional meaning of items, or words, in a syntactical structure is indicated by position—a change of position producing change of functional meaning. With an inflected language on the other hand it is the inflection, or *marker*—a term that will be more fully analysed in Chapter Three, which determines the functional meaning of the item in its context. A different function can be assigned to the same item only by altering its inflection, while a change of emphasis is all that is produced by altering the position of an item. This was shown in the case of:

meus amicus est sapiens

But the apparent simplicity of the point may mask its importance for successful learning of Latin, and even result in wrong emphasis being given to its various aspects so that its true significance is lost. In this text we shall frequently have occasion to remark on the importance of this point for stave analysis.

In English we are concerned with the whole of each word in a sentence. Although it has been found that the eye does not take in every letter of a word but only the shape or certain features of words as we read them, we are still concerned with both beginnings and ends in English.

In Latin, when the learner looks at a sentence, his first concern should not be with the stem of the words, since the stem is useful only for determining lexical meaning. The stem *Marc-* of *Marcus* indicates that the word has a different meaning from *Sextus* because of the different stem *Sext-*. Stems are important when we have recourse to the dictionary but are useless for giving information about the roles played by, for example, these two people in the action, or by any other representative words in a language context describing an action. Until the function of the Latin words has been determined, no recourse should be had to the dictionary to discover their equivalent meaning in English. The learner's first concern, therefore, when confronted with a Latin sentence is with the end (inflection) of each word rather than with its beginning (stem).

The functional meaning of the Latin words is shown by their inflections, or markers, which should stand out in clear relief to the eye of the learner. More will be said about the different nature and function of markers later in this text, but, for the moment marker will be used to indicate what is more usually referred to in Latin teaching as the word ending or inflection.

To show the marker, a skeleton sentence can be presented:

- - - -**us** - - - -**um** - - -**et**

Here each letter of the stem of the words in the original sentence is designated by a dash -. The marker indicates the role played by the word to which it is attached *in relation to all the other items or words in the context.*

The old adage 'look at the word ending' fails to emphasise this point since it rivets attention on the word whose ending is being 'looked at'. The marker on the other hand has both prospective and retrospective roles and never rivets attention on one particular place in the sentence.

The retrospective role is like the feedback mechanism in psychology; a marker of this type supplies, after forward movement of eye and mind indicated by a marker in a prospective role, further information referring back to that earlier marker.

If we apply the English reading technique of responding to each item from left to right as it appears in the sentence, we can derive considerable information from the markers of the skeleton sentence even though we may have no idea of the lexical meaning of the items. The first word is nominative (*–us* marker). The marker is prospective, anticipating a verb. The next marker *–um* is also forward looking since it is accusative, and, therefore, cannot be the verb. Thus we can say that the prospective *–um* reinforces the prospective idea of *–us*. But since the linguistic knowledge that even a young learner of Latin has tells him that accusatives are often recipients of actions from nominative subjects, the feedback already mentioned operates to connect *–us* and *–um*. The result of the original forward looking prompted by *–us* and the secondary prompting to look forward by *–um*, together with the connection ascertained by feedback between *–us* and *–um*—which, since it refers to, or suggests, an action, still requires a verb for its completion—sends the eye and mind forward to *–et*. This we recognise as a verb ending, and, more important, as a third person ending. Feedback again refers us to the nominative subject and perpetrator of an action, *–us*—and to the recipient of the action *–um*.

In terms of markers we can describe *–us* as an *opening* marker since it begins a process; *–et* as a *closing* marker since it ends a process begun by *–us*; and *–um* as a *secondary opening* marker, or *mediating* marker, since it confirms the information given by *–us* and mediates between *–us* and *–et*.

If we take the sentence in its second form, where we altered the order but not the markers of the words, the skeleton sentence appears as:

$$\text{- - - -um - - - -us - - -et}$$

This order of the words is important and should be borne in mind well beyond this chapter. For later, when more complex sentences are evaluated in terms of the markers of individual words, it will be shown that errors commonly occur when an accusative is the opening marker and the subject is delayed for up to twelve or more words.

It we return to consider adages and rules of thumb and the dangers they can introduce, we find that it is not uncommon for learners of Latin to be given the advice: 'look for the subject, look for the verb, look for the object'. While this rule in the case of the above sentence appears to present little danger, it will be shown to be pernicious and to lead to disaster where longer and more complex sentences are concerned.

If nothing else such advice is foolish linguistically, since in no language does the expert dart about hither and thither picking out isolated items from a mass of items. If the expert does not behave in this way, what reason is there for encouraging the learner so to behave, especially as the aim of teaching any language should be to make the learner expert in that language? Moreover, when the sentence contains subordinate clauses and in some cases a plethora of subjects, verbs and objects, it would be better had such advice never been given. Should this seem to overstate the case, we shall be looking at Latin sentences later where even the subject of the main sentences was not obvious to fifth formers asked to translate it. Finally, the advice initiates the undesirable excessive backward and forward movement of the eyes, which will be shown to introduce grave dangers.

In our second skeleton sentence:

$$\text{- - - -um - - - -us - - -et}$$

*–um* is the opening marker, and since it is object accusative it refers forward to a verb. *–us* does not constitute the marker for verb and is thus a secondary opening, or mediating, marker; it is prospective because it reminds us that the verb to whose presence *–um* alerted us has not been found, and by feedback we recognise that it is connected with *–um* in the same subject-object relation-

ship seen in the first skeleton sentence. Finally *–et* acts as closing marker as it did in the first example.

Two important points have emerged so far. First our concern with the *marker*, far from rivetting our attention on the word to which it is attached, refers us away from that word forward—and sometimes, through feedback, backwards—so that we assess each word in relation to the other words in the sentence. Secondly, although we are concerned with translating, in as much as we must ultimately consider what action the Latin words represent and how this may be expressed in English, we have not been concerned with lexical meaning. In our skeleton sentences such concern is impossible since we do not have the elements available from which to determine meaning. But we have, nevertheless, established the functional meaning of the words.

It is from failure to give the correct emphasis to these two points that teachers feel that a lacuna exists in the Latin course in the transition from the structured Latin of the course book to the unstructured writing of authors such as Livy, Caesar and Cicero. The old rules of thumb operate satisfactorily when applied to simple sentences and result in success—though the success following application of the rules is often not a matter of cause and effect but rather a case of post hoc ergo propter hoc. But because the rules do not produce success when the learner is required to translate complex sentences, teachers are compelled to seek another method of teaching translation. It is at this stage that the rift between grammar and translation, which up to now have proceeded pari passu, begins. The fault lies not in the Latin language but in teaching techniques employed in the early stages that are either faulty or are not techniques at all.

Once the structure of such a simple sentence as *Marcus Sextum videt* has been sufficiently emphasised—and no emphasis at this stage can be too great—the foundations will have been laid for more important and complex things. The moment one moves away from simple, one-clause sentences, one is likely to encounter the salient feature of Latin sentence structure; the *nesting* of one clause, or smaller unit of speech, within a larger unit of speech. Here the first dangers of 'look for the subject' look for the verb, look for the object' will be revealed.

It is not suggested that teachers of Latin do not lead their pupils from simple sentences to complex ones, nor that they give insufficient practice in translating both sentence types; it is the validity of the precepts that is being called into question here. One frequent fault arises when the pupil is taken from the simple sentence to the complex, and merely sees a long sentence containing mere words instead of a short sentence containing fewer words. The words still appear in lines of print of a conventional nature and the pupil is given no *visual* assistance to see the different shape of the syntactical structure. This visual assistance is provided by stave analysis.

Before the stave is explained there are further points to be considered. Let us take a sentence which is an expansion of a simple sentence like the one already examined and which the young learner soon encounters in his Latin course book:

Marcus magistri filius Sextum malum videt

Marcus, the schoolmaster's son, sees wicked Sextus

The complexity of this sentence is far from great by comparison with others shown later in this text but it can illustrate an idea vital to stave analysis: that the sentence can be reduced to our original one by removing two small *nesting units*. These are the units that supply the reader with more information, expand the basic information of the sentence, but do not change the basic information. Presenting the sentence in the form above will not bring out this vital point since it simply shows a sentence, about a situation perhaps already familiar, containing three more words. It is in the last fact that the danger lies.

The simplest way to reduce the sentence from its second (expanded) form to its simple (basic) form is to place brackets round the units that elaborate the original idea:

Marcus { magistri filius } Sextum { malum } videt

The markers are still presented in bold type, as they should be throughout the early stages of teaching if maximum benefit is to be derived from the stave presentation.

The pupil is here introduced to a convention with which he is already familiar in his study of mathematics: the bracket. He has been taught in his algebra lessons that he must always treat a bracket as a totality, that nothing may be removed from the bracket and associated with terms outside the bracket, and

26

that terms outside the bracket may not be absorbed into the bracket. The bracket is in essence sacrosanct and inviolable. Thus in the algebraic expression:

$$a+(b-c)+d$$

for purposes of evaluation the bracket $(b-c)$ constitutes a single term every bit as much as $a$ and $d$ do. At the stage of language study reached by the beginner learning Latin, the parallel between the brackets in the algebraic expression and the bracketed terms in the Latin sentence may not be immediately obvious. Consequently time spent making this point so clear that it will never thereafter be forgotten is time spent in the most valuable way possible. Thus if *magistri* in our example is removed from the sentence after being placed in the bracket then *filius* must be removed as well. If it is not, we perform an act equivalent to removing $b$ but not $c$ from the algebraic bracket[1].

The pupil must be given ample practice in expanding a basic structure by inserting brackets on the one hand, and removing brackets to produce a basic sentence by analytical methods on the other. Throughout the procedure visual assistance must be given to emphasise the function of analysis (reduction) and synthesis (expansion). These are vital preparations for the use of the stave.

The next type of sentence met is that expanded by the external addition of a dependent clause: for example:

hic Marcus est qui Romae habitat

This is Marcus, who lives in Rome

The danger here is that complex sentences may appear easy to deal with in Latin because, as in the example given above, the order of words is similar to that used in the English sentence expressing the same idea. However, the next sentence also uses an order similar to that of English but presents the young learner with greater difficulty, since the expansion of the basic sentence is produced internally by a nesting unit:

Marcus qui Romae habitat sapiens est

Marcus, who lives in Rome, is wise

[1] In later chapters it will be shown that a more refined analysis assigns both *magistri* and *filius* to separate brackets; but at the early stage the emphasis should be on the inviolability of brackets rather than on whether one or more brackets is warranted.

It is in translating sentences of this second type that the rule-of-thumb advice 'look for the subject, look for the verb, look for the object' is particularly dangerous. In this sentence there is no object but there are two subjects (one, the noun, much more easily recognisable than the relative pronoun which constitutes the other) and two verbs. The nesting of the complete bracket *qui Romae habitat* separates the first subject from its verb by the interposition of a three-word bracket. This circumstance was found to be the cause of breakdown in translation sense in complex Latin sentences met at fourth and fifth form level.

In the example above the sentence as a whole is reasonably short and both verbs are indicative. There is also only one interruption of the main sentence by a nesting unit, and the nesting unit is itself uninterrupted by further nesting units. In Chapters Three and Four it will be shown that the nesting of one unit within another can be multiplied indefinitely, necessitating a searching analysis to determine the limits of the nesting units. Further complications come when verbs appear in the subjunctive mood as well as in the indicative. The basic difficulty, however, appears long before sentences of such complexity are encountered.

It was found, as early as the first year of the Latin course, that boys who had never learned any of the standard syntactical constructions, if given any necessary vocabulary, could correctly translate the sentence:

Marcus **ad** for**um** ven**it ut** pan**em** emat

Marcus comes to the market to buy bread

However, not only were second formers completely unable to translate:

capt**ivi ut** sibi parc**eretur** statim ora**verunt**

The prisoners immediately begged to be spared

but also third and even fourth formers, who had learned the construction involved, were unable in many cases to produce anything approaching a correct translation. Yet there is no essential difference in pattern or structure between this sentence and

Marc**us qui** Romae habit**at** sapi**ens est**

Furthermore if the young learner has been taught the techniques illustrated so far (correct marker evaluation as distinct from looking at the word ending, and the use of brackets instead of looking haphazardly for subjects, verbs and objects) there is no reason why he should, at the proper stages in the course, find the first and the third of the above sentences comparatively easy to translate but the second impossibly difficult.

In the sentences:

Marcus **qui** Romae habitat sapi**ens est**

captivi **ut** sibi parceretur statim orav**erunt**

there is one factor common to both: the separation of the beginning of the basic information content from the end by the use of a further information-giving unit. In the sentence:

**hic** Marc**us est qui** Romae habitat

the expanding unit is added at the end of the basic information-giving unit; but in the first two sentences quoted above it is so added that it nests within the main unit. Visual assistance should supplement the verbal explanation given to the pupils when this fact is explained. The basic information, as well as the additional information, can be placed in separate linguistic brackets, and the subsidiary information brackets can be inserted and removed *in toto*. The brackets for the sentences above are:

**hic** Marc**us est** {**qui** Romae habitat}

captivi orav**erunt** {statim} {**ut** sibi parceretur}

Marcus sapi**ens est** {**qui** Romae habitat}

The final sentence was, after insertion or addition without violation of any bracket, presented in the form:

Marcus {**qui** Romae habitat} sapi**ens est**

while

    captivi orav**erunt**

    {statim}

    {**ut** sibi parceretur}

was presented in the form:

captivi {**ut** sibi parc**eretur**} {statim} orav**erunt**

This last sentence was set as part of a research test battery for third and fourth formers, i.e. pupils in their second and third years of the Latin course. Serious mistranslations occurred, of which three examples are given:

He spared the prisoners and immediately begged himself

At once the prisoners themselves spared and begged

He spared the prisoners who at once begged themselves

Latin teachers will doubtless be familiar with this type of result. Further research with a large sample of eight hundred pupils from sixteen schools showed that similar breakdown in translation sense occurred as late as the fifth form (the fourth year of Latin) when pupils are entered for the 'O' level examination, some sixty per cent of which usually consists of translation from Latin into English.

There are two causes of such serious breakdown. The first is failure to isolate the linguistic bracket and to keep the content of that bracket inviolate; the second is failure to make the correct response to the markers. Later in this text it will become clear how these failures are interconnected.

The markers in the sentence under consideration fall into two categories: the *inflection marker*, already seen in simple sentences relating each word to the other words in the structure, and the *dependence markers* that set the parameters within which the inflection markers are evaluated. Examples of dependence markers are **ut**, and the **–eretur** of *parceretur*. These are a linguistic indication of the limits of dependent units, which have been schematically represented by the brackets. Bracket, or unit, violation, and the assimilation of part of the content of one bracket to another bracket to which it does not belong, thus causing further violation, is the prime cause of the gross translation error that stave analysis was designed to eliminate.

While the function of individual Latin words is indicated not by their physical position in a sentence but by markers, the physical position of brackets in relation to other brackets is vitally important. This will later be seen as a key factor in stave analysis.

Zellig Harris[1] comes to a similar conclusion when he analyses English sentences into constituent *strings* in much the same way as we have done with brackets. Harris does not attach a technical definition to each string—a common practice in sentence analysis in English grammar lessons condemned by Fries as unproductive;[2] instead he refers to the strings as adjuncts to the right or to the left of other words or strings of words, a

[1]*String Analysis of Sentence Structure*, p. 9 et seq.
[2]*The Structure of English*, p. 55.

point which will be considered again in Chapter Five. Thus the sentence:

The man who was wearing an overcoat caught the bus

would be analysed into the following strings:

| | |
|---|---|
| *man caught bus* | elementary sentence |
| *the* | adjunct to the left of *man* |
| *who was wearing overcoat* | adjunct to the right of *man* |
| *an* | adjunct to the left of *overcoat* |
| *the* | adjunct to the left of *bus* |

The adjunct *who was wearing (an) overcoat*, which is to the right of *man* and is directly connected in a syntactical sense to it, could be placed in brackets. This would indicate that none of its constituent items could be removed and associated with items in other brackets not directly related to it syntactically, and that it could not be moved as a whole without altering, or even destroying, the sense of the sentence. Consequently it could not be placed to the right of *bus*, the hierarchical structure of the sentence forbidding such an interruption.

This last point is easily appreciated by the English reader because it relates to an English sentence whose meaning he understands immediately. He knows that it is nonsense to talk about a *bus* wearing *an overcoat*. But the situation for the Englishman, who can read and readily interpret the meaning of an English sentence, alters when he is confronted with the problem of reading a Latin sentence; here he does not understand the sentence before he analyses it. And, as the analysis is carried out to help derive the meaning or information content, it cannot be condemned as an unproductive exercise.

Since the English sentence referring to the *man* and the *bus* is analysed in terms of English words, the Latin sentence must be analysed in terms of the Latin words. It should not be analysed in terms of English equivalents of the Latin words, nor, worse still, of a combination of some Latin words and some English equivalents. The primary concern must be with Latin structure, not with lexical meaning in English.

The sentence *Marcus qui Romae habitat sapiens est* highlights another feature of the reading process, which is also apparent from the English translation *Marcus, who lives at Rome, is wise.* This is that when the reader in the mother tongue looks at a sentence with the idea of deriving information from it, his mind frequently has to suspend judgement in response to a marker or markers. In the English translation of this Latin sentence, we know from the first word that somebody called *Marcus* features somehow in an action or a state of being. When we come to *who* we are told that a bracket is beginning and interrupting the main flow and main information content of the sentence. The marker *who* informs us that the bracket will tell us more about *Marcus*, but it will not give us the main information about him that the sentence is designed to convey. We know this because main information does not appear in a unit which nests within the main unit, although a nesting unit may expand basic information. The same response should be made to the marker *qui* in the Latin sentence. This suspending of judgement is important for appreciating the significance of word order.

We have seen that the English-speaking learner can analyse an English sentence in terms of known meaning. We have also compared English and Latin sentences, but we have not so far revealed the magnitude of the problem in Latin because the English sentences quoted posed no great difficulty. A more striking comparison is afforded by the English child confronted with a piece of English verse and with a piece of Latin prose or, still more striking, with a piece of Latin verse.

Teachers of Latin and English frequently state that pupils are unable to understand the meaning of verse because the ideas expressed are too difficult. This is a convenient explanation but not necessarily accurate: in some cases, especially in narrative poetry in Latin, it constitutes another misconception. In many cases the problem is basically a linguistic one, and could be classified as a 'word-order problem' with characteristics in common with such sentences as *captivi ut sibi parceretur statim oraverunt*. While more complex verbal structures could be found in English than the four lines below from *The Charge of the Light Brigade*, these were chosen because they convey an idea easily grasped by the young reader, but still illustrate the linguistic problem posed by a word order that is unusual when compared with the prose of everyday English, and show how judgement must be suspended:

Half a league, half a league,
Half a league onward
Into the Valley of Death
Rode the Six Hundred.

No functional sense, and consequently no real meaning, can be derived from the words *half a league* at the beginning until the words *rode the Six Hundred* at the end of the verse have been evaluated. The mind of the reader responds to the signal which the early words give, and suspends judgement pending more information. By a definition already established, *half a league* is an opening marker and *rode* and *the Six Hundred* are closing markers. When the closing markers are seen, the mind responds by feedback to the opening markers and reaches the position where it is able to assign meaning to the whole verse. However, as the English reader is skilled in responding to signals and markers in English, he does not have to make his eye travel back to the opening markers, because, once his mind has responded to them and suspended judgement, it carries the information with it as it responds to the remaining markers.

From this emerge two points relevant to translation from Latin into English. First, the practice equivalent to looking up the lexical meaning of *half* and *league* immediately these words are seen, and before the eye has travelled to the end of the verse and before the mind has evaluated all the markers, opening, secondary (mediating) and closing, is shown to be futile. Secondly, when the translator from Latin perceives the beginning of a bracket through the marker of dependence opening the bracket, his mind must suspend judgement until a dependence marker is encountered which closes the bracket. Once the bracket has been closed, the ongoing sense, which the bracket temporarily interrupted, is often resumed.

Suspending judgement may be a long and complex task. This is illustrated by the Latin sentence below, which is presented first as it appears on a page of standard print and then with brackets inserted:[1]

[1]This analysis using brackets is simple. For a more complex analysis, and a translation of this sentence, see p. 73.

postero die cum per exploratores cognovisset quo in loco
hostes qui Brundisio profecti erant castra posuissent
flumen transgressus est ut hostes extra moenia vagantes
et nullis custodibus positis incautos ante solis occasum
aggrederetur

{postero die} {cum [per exploratores] cognovisset [quo
in loco hostes ⟨qui Brundisio profecti erant⟩ castra
posuissent]} flumen transgressus est {ut hostes
[extra moenia] vagantes et [nullis custodibus positis]
incautos [ante solis occasum] aggrederetur}

The complexity of such a sentence caused by the number of
linguistic units in its hierarchical structure, many of which nest
within larger units which are themselves already nesting, makes
the use of brackets of different shapes desirable if the various
units are to be correctly delineated and easily perceived. In
complex sentences as in simple ones, only dependent units are
enclosed within brackets, thus reducing the complex to the
elementary sentence—which does not appear within brackets of
any kind. In this text the shape { is used to open and } to close
the first and any subsequent first-order dependent block to be
encountered. Should any block be found to nest within a first-
order dependent block, it is indicated by the bracket shape [ ];
further units which nest within previous units are delineated
by the shape ⟨ ⟩ for third-order dependence and ( ) for fourth-
order dependence, to produce on the fullest analysis the strict
sequence for nesting units of

$$\{ \, [ \, \langle \, ( \qquad ) \, \rangle \, ] \, \}$$

Since nesting can be carried on to the $n$th order of dependence
(see page 62), $n$ pairs of diversely shaped brackets could, in
theory, be required. However, it will be seen that the four
bracket shapes shown above will be sufficient for many complex
sentences, including all the sentences introduced into this text
for analysis except for the sentence on page 58.

Clearly much bracketing and suspending judgement must be
undertaken in this example before the 'elementary sentence'
(Harris's definition) *flumen transgressus est* is isolated. Even more
bracketing intervenes before the elementary sentence can be
expanded into the main plus secondary information content,
represented by:

flumen transgressus est ut hostes aggrederetur

The key markers, both of word inflection and of dependence, are set in bold type to show the correspondence that exists between them and the opening and closing of brackets. In the next chapter it will be shown that the technique necessary to analyse this complex sentence is only a logical extension of the simple technique used with

Marcus Sextum videt

Indeed the sentence *flumen transgressus est* is no more complex than *Marcus Sextum videt*; it becomes complex only when expanded, a process that could equally be applied to the *Marcus* sentence.

In the next chapter we shall employ, using a sentence as complex as the one analysed above, the technique of responding to each inflection marker and dependence marker as it appears in linear progression on the printed page as opposed to letting the eye dart back and forth looking for subjects, verbs and objects. In successfully demonstrating the effectiveness of this method we shall substantiate our point that there need be no difference in technique employed in translating simple and complex Latin sentences. We shall also show that no lacuna caused by the language need ever be felt; such lacuna are the result of wrong techniques of teaching translation in the initial stages of learning.

It is too late to introduce techniques such as bracketing and marker evaluation when complex sentences are met. By this time the pupil taught by rule-of-thumb methods will have formed many incorrect habits. The crossing of markers which delineate the limits of linguistic brackets without realising their significance is one of the worst and stems directly from the undue eye movement produced by looking for subjects, verbs and objects. The value of the approach proposed here is missed by the pupil because the application of rules of thumb will have resulted in an item-centred rather than a structure-centred approach to translation.

At the stage when the complex sentence is reached, the rule of thumb is altered, producing advice that is equally injurious. usually in the form: 'isolate the main clause first'. Not only is it difficult to see what value there is in this exercise, or how such isolation shall be accomplished, but what reader of his native tongue would ever undertake so linguistically naïve an exercise?

Thus, we are brought right back to a point made in the first chapter: that, if translation is to serve a real purpose, it must provide the final step in the process leading to the ability to read. This can be achieved only on deciding what is to be learned in the reading process. To do this, we must examine and make conscious the thought processes which the reader employs unconsciously and automatically. This is what stave analysis does. The young learner of Latin *sees* the processes because they are visually presented to him; gradually he *internalises* these processes; and when the responses which constitute the process become automatic and unconsciously performed, he has perfected the skill we call reading.

## Chapter Three

# THE IMPORTANCE OF LINGUISTIC MARKERS
# IN LATIN

A DISCUSSION of all the types and functions of linguistic markers is beyond the compass of the present text. Readers who are interested in pursuing the matter in greater depth are referred to the work of W. Hass.[1] Our main concern is with the use of markers in stave analysis and in the work of the Latin course connected with stave analysis.

In the last chapter we established that there are two main types of markers. First, in simple sentences, there is the *inflection* of each item; this indicates the role of that item in relation to the other items in the total structure, enabling the reader, or translator, to evaluate the items in turn without altering the order in which they appear. Secondly, both the inflection markers and *dependence* markers occur in complex sentences; these make possible the accurate delineation of linguistic brackets which nest within the total sentence structure, and whose aggregate makes up the syntactical hierarchy of the complex sentence. The dependence marker may be a whole word, such as *ut* or *cum*, *qui* or *si*, or it may be an inflection marker used in conjunction with a whole-word marker of dependence. Such markers indicate the limits and essential characteristic of the unit of speech within the bracket.

In the three sentences below the whole-word and inflection markers of dependence are printed in bold type:

ad forum **ut** panem em**eret** iit
He went to the market to buy bread

Marcus **qui** Romae habit**at** sapiens est
Marcus, who lives in Rome, is wise

[1]*Linguistic Relevance*, one of a series of essays in *In Memory of J. R. Firth* (see bibliography).

**cum** ad urbem ven**isset** mortuus est
When he came to the city he died

In the first two sentences the dependent unit nests within the main unit while in the third sentence it is added externally, before the elementary sentence, although it could equally well follow the elementary sentence.[1] Yet in every case the reader or translator must have precise criteria for bracket delineation if bracket violation—and the subsequent assimilation of part of the violated bracket to the content of another bracket with which it is not directly connected syntactically—is to be avoided.

The markers of dependence indicated above fall into the two categories already defined as *opening* and *closing* markers. The opening marker begins a unit of speech, and, as well as operating by feedback to the word or string of words[2] to the left or right of which the adjunct or bracket lies, warn the translator to suspend judgement until a *closing* marker is found that replies to the opening marker in a way experience has taught him to expect. Closing markers of nesting brackets indicate that the line of thought interrupted by the nesting of a dependent unit may be resumed.

Trubetskoy,[3] writing about *Grenzsignale*, or boundary signals, states that these can be likened to traffic lights in a busy, modern city. Just as the traffic lights warn the motorist that he may proceed or that he must stop or that it is necessary to continue with caution, so the Grenzsignale give similar warnings to the reader. The markers of dependence are not necessarily exactly identified with Grenzsignale in the sense meant by Trubetskoy, but their function is essentially the same. If the reader or translator does not find himself halting in his linear progress through the sentence shown below when the marker *ut* appears, he ought at least to find himself proceeding with caution:

urbem **ut** hostes de**lerent** incenderunt
They set fire to the city to destroy the enemy

Some markers have different functions in different grammatical situations and accordingly the learner has to come to exercise care. Thus in the first year of the Latin course the learner is

---

[1]But in that case ven**isset** would become indicative.
[2]See page 31 et seq.
[3]*Grundzüge der Phonologie*, p. 255.

taught that *cum* is a preposition followed by the ablative case and means *with* (accompanied by) as in:

He went **with** Marcus

cum Marco iit

as distinct from *with* (instrumental):

He killed Marcus **with** a stone

Marcum lapide necavit

Later he must learn that *cum* in a different grammatical situation may be followed by particular tenses of the subjunctive and that this denotes 'when in past time', 'although', since'. In yet another grammatical situation *cum* may be the opening marker which is closed by an indicative, where it can mean 'whenever'. Consequently it is unwise to make a snap decision about the function of *cum* as a marker. In may be doubly unwise in an ambiguous situation when a word, in the case that *cum* meaning 'with' requires for closure, follows immediately after *cum* but is not in fact the closing marker. For example:

**cum** custodibus positis ex castris **isset**

When, after posting sentries, he went out from the camp

This illustrates that both the simple item inflection marker and the marker of syntactical dependence function as traffic lights for the reader, and—even more pertinently—for the translator, if he is to obtain safe passage through a syntactical complex. Some markers are more important than others since more depends on them, and a wrong turning at these may well lead to gross error. Sometimes such a marker stands in a strategic position in a main clause without seeming at first glance to be of outstanding importance, as -*o* of Brut*o* in:

Brut*o* media nocte cum adlato lumine solus res varias mente agitaret atra imago se obtulit et cum Brutus rogasset quae esset imago 'tuus' inquit 'malus genius'

A black ghost appeared to Brutus in the middle of the night when, having fetched a lamp, he was turning various matters over in his mind in solitude, and when Brutus asked what it was the ghost said, 'Your evil spirit'.

In this position *Bruto* is a double trap for the unwary translator. It stands precisely where the subject commonly stands in English, and not uncommonly in Latin. Furthermore a superficial glance—which may be all that the catchphrase 'seeing one's way through the sentence' means on many occasions—indicates that Brutus is, indeed, the perpetrator of actions throughout the sentence. If later, why not sooner? It is not easy for the inexperienced translator unaccustomed to the importance of markers to account for the case of *Bruto*; this involves recognising -*o* as opening marker for which *obtulit* is the closing marker, since *offerre*[1] is a verb requiring a dative for its own completion. The connection is not made any the more obvious by the thirteen items intervening between the opening and the closing markers.

Such a sentence is a severe test of the translator's ability to suspend judgement. But if this is not done the danger is cumulative and the units of dependence which follow are imperilled, even before the opening marker of the first one is reached. The translator, unable to account for the case of *Bruto*, ignores the marker and translates it ad sensum as subject; he does this not because he is ignorant of the fact that the subject can never appear in the dative case, but because he cannot make sense of the sentence with *Bruto* correctly evaluated as dative. He regresses to behaviour that has previously brought success in English and Latin, and takes the first word in the sentence as subject. Thus committed wrongly he finds other dangers following.

The *cum*, which is opening marker to *agitaret*, is taken as closed by *adlato lumine* for reasons shown above.

Once embarked on this road to disaster, the translator ignores or misinterprets marker after marker and presents as his translation an ad sensum completion to an originally wrong idea. 'Look for the subject, look for the verb, look for the object' and 'isolate the main clause first' are treacherous allies in this situation. More will be said later in this chapter about the difficulty resulting from the delayed appearance of the subject after a series of markers indicating oblique cases.

Secondary or mediating markers are also important for our case. These are inflection markers which, far from closing the opening marker, serve as a reminder to the reader or translator that a unit of speech has been opened, and instruct him to be on

---

[1]Offero, offerre, obtuli, oblatum: the double *f* is derived from the combination of the prefix *ob* with *fero*: 'obfero' (offero).

the lookout for a closing marker. Their function is limited to a context smaller than the total sentence, after one of the parameters of the context has been set by the opening marker. In the field of learning theory Hull denies that every action can be regarded as a simple response to a simple stimulus.[1] The rat running the maze is a case in point; it does not, according to Hull, make one response but a series of fractional anticipatory goal responses between its initial response of starting to run the maze and its final response, finding food at the far end of the maze. Thus running a maze is a complex chain of actions or behaviours. Similarly the translator or reader does not make a single response to an opening marker, followed by another single response to a closing marker. The secondary (mediating) markers[2] between the opening and closing markers evoke responses similar to the fractional anticipatory goal responses made by Hull's rats. It may be necessary, because of the length and complexity of certain sentences, to give the translator a second, third, fourth up to an $n$th reminder that a unit of speech has been begun (opened) but not completed (closed).

In view of what has been said so far about the nature of linguistic markers and of complex Latin sentences, it is apparent that there are two types of sentences and two main categories of markers which require attention.

The types of marker are:
    (i) the simple inflection marker of individual items indicating the grammatical interrelationship of all the internal constituents of the structure,

and (ii) the markers of dependence which are the parameters setting the limits of structure, and within which all evaluation of inflection markers must take place.

---

[1]Clark, L. Hull (1884–1952): an American behaviourist psychologist of the Guthrie, Skinner school. His theory of learning is purely mechanistic and eschews such subjective ideas as mind, consciousness, thinking, etc. The central factor of his learning theory is habit, and he regards the most complex behaviour as derived from simple behaviour. His 'habit family hierarchy' enables the learner to make the optimum use of past learning experience in a new learning situation.

[2]Similarly, co-ordinating markers (e.g. *atque* p. 43, and *que* p. 55 et seq.) are a reminder that two units of equal value are directly linked. In the example on p. 55, *que* really stands for a second *cum* and is equal in value to the first *cum*.

The two main types of complex sentence are:
> (i) those which, although complex, and in some instances containing nesting units, do not contain nesting units which are syntactically dependent constructions,

and (ii) the type of sentence where the nesting units are syntactically dependent constructions.

Our research has shown that both types of complex sentences can cause difficulty for the unwary or the unskilled translator. Both types of sentence require a structural analysis in terms of inflection and/or dependence markers, with responses made to each word in its order in the Latin sentence.

An analysis showing every response made is given below. The reactions are those which the learner taught by linguistic methods will make in the early stages of translating complex Latin. As his experience and competence increase he will reduce the number of responses since some will become superfluous. This is true of learning any skill and is essential if progress is to be made. The reader—as distinct from the translator—will also make some of the responses indicated in the course of the analysis but his mind will make them unconsciously. The acts presented below are meant to be exhaustive purely for purposes of illustration, and to pave the way for an explanation of stave analysis. These are the responses the teacher will show the learner and which he will subsequently require the learner to perform for himself, at first aloud, as in reading aloud, and then silently as a result of the internalisation of a learned process.

The first example is of a complex sentence without nesting syntactical constructions, but whose subject is introduced only after a series of words in oblique cases and is not easily recognisable as the subject.[1] The sentence is from Livy:
> evaden**tem** per for**um** atque effugien**tem** regi**i** satellit**es** correp**tum ad** reg**em** traxer**unt**
>
> The king's minions seized him as he was slipping away through the forum and making his escape, and haled him before the king.

The following analysis is an exhaustive account of the behavioural steps of the learner:

[1]Type (i), above.

*evadentem*

*–em* is an opening marker denoting accusative singular. Since it is accusative, the word represents the recipient of the action of a verb, and alerts the translator to wait for a verb. Judgement must be suspended until more information is available.[1]

*per*

This cannot be a closing marker to *evadentem* since it is not a verb, and *per* requires an accusative for its own completion.

It cannot be closed by the accusative *evadentem* since prepositions are used in anastrophe, i.e. following their noun or closing marker, only by verse writers such as Vergil. If this marker is independent of the *–em* of *evadentem* it can only be a mediating marker in its secondary role.[2] The only possible alternative is that it interrupts the sense of the simple sentence, opening a bracket. Thus we have so far:

      evadentem {per . . .

*forum*

The *-um* marker indicates accusative singular. Since the ongoing sense has been interrupted by *per* opening a bracket, *–um* cannot be a secondary (mediating) marker to *cum*. It must, therefore, be the closing marker required to complete the structural sense of *per*. Thus the bracket is closed and a unit,

      {per forum}

is completed, giving:

      evadentem {per forum} . . .

*atque*

Co-ordinating marker.[3] In this position it could be resuming the ongoing sense interrupted by *per forum*, thus acting

---

[1] The similarity between this and the - - - *um* - - - *us* - - - *et* in Chapter Two should be noted.

[2] It is important to note that a marker whose primary role is that of opening a small nesting unit of speech acts, in its secondary role, as a reminder that the opening marker of the larger unit in which it nests has still to be closed.

[3] p. 46 footnote.

as co-ordinator between *evadentem* and some word yet to come; or, feasibly, between *forum* and some word yet to come, in which case closing the nesting bracket after *forum* would be premature. As further information is required, judgement must be suspended.

      evadent**em** {**per** forum **atque** . . .

### effugientem

The **–em** marker denotes accusative singular. It now appears likely that **atque** co-ordinates the pair that *evadentem* and *effugientem* form. It it should be acting as a co-ordinator between *forum* and *effugientem*, **–em** of *effugientem* must be a second, secondary or mediating marker, serving as a reminder that the functional sense of *evadentem* has yet to be determined. Taking **atque** as co-ordinating marker for *evadentem* and *effugientem* we have:

      evadent**em** {**per** forum} **atque** effugient**em** . . .

This confirms by feedback the closing of *per* by *forum*.

### regii

The marker **ii** is less definite than those so far encountered. It denotes either genitive singular or nominative plural. As it does not in either case act as closing marker to the accusatives, it may be regarded as a secondary (mediating) marker. Should it denote the beginning of a bracket it will be another opening marker.

Suspension of judgement pending further information is needed.

Schematic representation of sentence analysis up to this point shows:

      evadent**em** {**per** forum} **atque** effugient**em** regii

or:

      evadent**em** {**per** forum} **atque** effugient**em** {regii

### satellites

The **–es** marker could denote either nominative or accusative plural. As **–ii** of *regii* could be nominative plural, there might well be a nominative pair:

      reg**ii** satellit**es** *or* {regii} satellit**es**—(adjective) noun forming the subject of a verb yet to appear. If this were so, there might be a connection by feedback between this subject of the verb and the recipient of the action of a verb indicated by

evadent**em atque** effugient**em**

In this case we should have further secondary markers indicating that additional information was required. The analysis would be:

evadent**em** {**per** for**um**} **atque** effugient**em** {reg**ii**} satellit**es** . . .

*correptum*

The *–um* marker is accusative singular and refers back to the previous accusative singular markers *–em*. This is yet another secondary, marker, resuming after

evadent**em atque** effugient**em**

and it now appears that *regii satellites*, or {*regii*} *satellites*, are the perpetrators of some action on

evadent**em atque** effugient**em** corrept**um**

and that *evadentem atque effugientem* qualifies *correptum* and hence can be placed in a bracket. *Per forum* gives more information about the direction of *evadentem* but cannot be directly connected with it—as *effugientem* is—because it forms part of a nesting bracket with *per*.

*ad*

This marker is similar to *per*. It requires an accusative closing marker, which cannot be the *–um* of *correptum* just as *evadentem* earlier could not be closing marker for *per*. It indicates the start of another interruption in the main sentence flow—the start of another nesting bracket.

{evadent**em** [**per** for**um**] **atque** effugient**em**} {reg**ii**} satellit**es** corrept**um** {**ad** . . .

*regem*

The *–em* marker denotes accusative singular and closes *ad*, giving a small nesting bracket

**ad** reg**em**

{evadent**em** [**per** for**um**] **atque** effugient**em**} {reg**ii**} satellit**es** corrept**um** {**ad** reg**em**} . . .

*traxerunt*

This is a verb, perfect tense, indicative, third person plural. It acts, by feedback, as a closing marker to the original opening marker *–em* of *evadentem* and to all subsequent secondary (mediating) and co-ordinating markers of accusative and nominative case. Consequently it is the closing marker to the *–ii* and to the *–es* (which it finally establishes beyond doubt as nominative) of

{reg**ii**} satell**ites,**

the adjective-noun combination acting as subject to the verb. The closing marker links the perpetrator of the action (grammatical subject) with the recipient of the action (grammatical object) in the form of:

{evadent**em atque** effugient**em**} . . . . . . corrept**um**

Thus the basic information is given in the elementary sentence:

satell**ites** corrept**um** trax**erunt**

If the brackets are reinserted we have the following presentation:

{evadent**em** [**per** for**um**] **atque** effugient**em**}  {reg**ii**} satell**ites** corrept**um** {**ad** reg**em**} trax**erunt.**

It should be noted that *correptum* rather than *evadentem* or *effugientem* is in the elementary sentence because of a peculiar Latin idiom. We say: 'They *seized* the *man* and *haled him* . . .', using two finite verbs; Latin dispenses with 'the man' and says: 'They haled the having been seized man'. Therefore we have, by expansion:The {King's} minions haled {before the king{ the having been seized man {slipping [through the forum] and escaping}

Sentences of this type are difficult for the translator because they are structurally amorphous compared with the commoner type of sentence beginning with a clearly defined subject and ending with a clearly defined verb. This problem will be considered again when sentences with different hierarchical structures are subjected to stave analysis.

Another sentence from the research battery, which caused difficulty for similar reasons, also came from Livy:

hic in propinquis urbi montibus moratus expedivit se exercitus

> here the army, tarrying in the mountains hard by the city, made its preparations

The danger here is presented by the opening marker *hic*. This looks like the familiar, nominative, masculine singular form of the demonstrative pronoun, representing the subject and placed in an appropriate position. In fact it is the adverbial *hic* meaning 'here'. However, the translator soon finds himself in difficulties with the interrupting bracket

> in propinquis {urbi} montibus

where the speech pattern is different from the English

> in the mountains close by the city

Many pupils translated *urbi* as genitive. The psychological explanation for this (which was also revealed by our research) is both interesting and important. Piaget talks about the formation of a schema or series of schemata when the child learns. A schema is a more or less well-organised behaviour sequence in response to a stimulus complex. In the early days of Latin learning, when second declension nouns are learned (and the learning later reinforced and practised), it is established that *-i* is the inflection marker for the genitive singular (2nd declension):

| | | | |
|---|---|---|---|
| *magister* | the school master | *magistri* | of the school master |
| *bellum* | war | *belli* | of the war |

A schema is formed and the learned material practised.

Later, when the third declension is learned, the child finds that *-i* is now an inflection marker denoting dative singular:

| | | | |
|---|---|---|---|
| *urbs* | city | *urbi* | to or for the city |

But earlier formed schemata are better organised than later formed schemata because the material learned has been practised more frequently. Under pressure the translator 'assimilates' the less well-organised to the better-organised schema—in this case from third declension dative to second declension genitive. The same phenomena are manifest in the confusion of such perceptually similar words as:

| | |
|---|---|
| *constitit* | he halted (less well-organised schema) |
| and *constituit* | he decided (better organised) |
| *sus* | a pig (less well organised) |
| and *suus* | his or her (better organised) |

47

<pre>
    hostia          sacrificial victim (less well organised)
and hostes          enemy (better organised)
</pre>

and in errors of copying in classical manuscripts. In this last instance we always substitute (when emendations are made to a corrupt manuscript) the more difficult for the simpler reading. The copier 'assimilated' the less well-organised schema (correct reading) to a better-organised schema (the easier, incorrect reading).

Matters are further complicated after the closure of the bracket by the participle *moratus* agreeing with *exercitus*; this precedes the noun in the sentence and is separated from it by a reflexive verb—which, unusual in Latin, precedes its own subject.[1]

> hic in propinquis urbi montibus moratus expedivit se exercitus

Bracketing gives:

> {hic [in ⟨propinquis (urbi)⟩ montibus]} {moratus} expedivit se exercitus

This reveals the elementary sentence:

> expedivit se exercitus
> the army prepared itself

expandable, unit by unit, as follows:

> {hic} expedivit se exercitus
> {here} the army prepared itself
> {hic} {moratus} expedivit se exercitus
> {tarrying} {here} the army prepared itself
> {hic [in montibus]} {moratus} expedivit se exercitus
> {tarrying} {here [in the mountains]} the army prepared itself
> {hic [in ⟨propinquis⟩ montibus]} {moratus} expedivit se exercitus
> {tarrying} {here [in the mountains ⟨hard by⟩]} the army prepared itself
> {hic [in ⟨propinquis (urbi)⟩ montibus]} {moratus} expedivit se exercitus
> {tarrying} {here [in the mountains ⟨hard by (the city)⟩]} the army prepared itself

[1]For a similar example in a dependent clause see *erupissent hostes*, p. 56.

The relative position of the brackets in the Latin and English sentences illustrates the different word orders in the two languages and the contrastive speech patterns used.

In such sentences the translator, while he is inexperienced, should tread still more warily, to the extent of examining every linguistically possible alternative of every word. One false marker evaluation leads immediately to error and ultimately to random behaviour and to complete breakdown of sense.

The *evadentem* sentence above, although difficult as it stands, may be rendered even more difficult by indefinite expansion. One well-known sentence from Livy beginning very much like the *evadentem* sentence, is so expanded; after much bracketing and nesting of units inside other units, it suddenly ends on a note of anticlimax with a simple four item main clause. This sentence was also included in the test battery for the research and is presented below, together with a detailed analysis. It is an example of a type (ii) complex sentence described on page 42 since, unlike the *evadentem* sentence, the expansion occurs through the addition of syntactical constructions.

> cum subito exercitum Romanum Coriolos obsidentem atque in oppidanos quos intus clausos habebat intentum sine ullo metu extrinsecus imminentis belli Volscae legiones profectae ab Antio invasissent eodemque tempore ex oppido erupissent hostes forte in statione Marcus fuit.

A rule-of-thumb approach to such a complex is indefensible. The only hope is to proceed word by word responding correctly to markers; these may show the inflection of items in relation to other items, or may be markers of dependence indicating the opening and closing of brackets that are frequently nesting. Such a technique will ultimately reveal the structural shape of the sentence:

### *cum*

Opening marker, requiring ablative, subjunctive, or indicative for closure. It is probable that *cum* opens a dependent unit: it would always be dependent and hence require an opening bracket, if it introduced a clause. However, even if it only governed a noun in the ablative case, strict analysis would almost certainly bracket it off from the main clause.[1]

## subito

Secondary marker. It cannot close *cum* because it fulfils none of the requirements postulated above. It therefore mediates between *cum* and its closing marker. As it is an adverb *subito* may be placed in a bracket since it can do no more than simply expand the basic sense of its verb, when this is revealed by progress through the sentence.

## exercitum

The *–um* denotes accusative. It cannot close *cum* and is therefore a secondary (mediating) marker warning the reader by its case to look for a verb. This might be subjunctive as the closing marker to *cum*, perpetrating an action on *exercitum*.

{cum [subito] exercitum . . .

## Romanum

Another accusative, associated by feedback with *exercitum*, and, like *exercitum*, a secondary marker.

## Coriolos

*–os* indicates accusative plural. It neither closes *cum* nor can it be associated by feedback with *exercitum*, which is singular. It is, therefore, forward looking (mediating), reminding the reader or translator to suspend judgement still longer. It presents, for the moment, a difficult problem.

## obsidentem

*–em* denotes accusative singular and by feedback becomes associated with *exercitum* and *Romanum*. Thus it is a closing marker to a small unit, the last three words of which expand the first:

exercitum Romanum Coriolos obsidentem.

It also has the function of a secondary marker since it

---

[1] E.g. (*Cum Marco*) *Romam iit. Cum Marco* could never be part of a strict elementary sentence in this aspect.

50

reminds us that *cum* has still not been answered by a closing marker. In the previous sentence

in propinquis urbi montibus

caused difficulty by the position of *propinquis*, which made functional and structural sense only when completed by *montibus*. In rather similar fashion *Coriolos* causes difficulty until the functional and structural sense is competed by *obsidentem*:

{cum [subito] exercit**um** [Roman**um**] Coriol**os** obsidentem

Since *Coriolos obsidentem* (like *Romanum*) gives additional information about *exercitum*, it also could be bracketed:

exercit**um** [Roman**um**] [Coriol**os** obsidentem]

*atque*

This conjunction is a co-ordinating[1] marker and alerts the translator to the possibility of further expansion to the unit

exercit**um** Roman**um** Coriol**os** obsidentem

Conjunctions are strictly described as 'co-ordinating' markers, though their function (as here) can often be defined as that of mediating between two units, small or large.

*in*

Opening marker. It cannot follow upon **atque**. It requires an accusative for its own closure, and consequently is an interruption of the ongoing sentence. It does, however, function as a mediating marker reminding the reader or translator that the opening marker **cum** has not been closed.

{cum [subito] exercit**um** [Roman**um**] Coriol**os** obsidentem atque [in . . .

*oppidanos*

–**os** is the closing marker to **in**. As the unit

in oppidan**os**

has no functional meaning in relation to what has gone before, it cannot be placed in a bracket—unlike **per forum**

---

[1]Note the similarity between *obsidentem* **atque** . . . *intentum* (p. 53) and *evadentem* **atque** *effugientem* (p. 45), albeit in the former case the nesting interruption is much greater.

which followed *evadentem* in a previous example. *Oppidanos* cannot be taken directly with *Coriolos* because of the intervention of **in** which interrupts the ongoing sense after the co-ordinating **atque**. Judgement has still to be suspended.

### quos

This is related by feedback to *oppidanos*, but is also the opening marker to a relative clause and consequently opens another bracket.

There has still been no closing marker for **cum** so that **quos** is both opening marker to its own bracket and mediating marker (secondary role) after **cum**.

{**cum** [subito] exercitum [Romanum] Coriolos obsidentem atque [in oppidanos ⟨quos . . .

### intus

This is a secondary mediating marker between **quos** and a verb yet to come. It does not close **quos**. It is an adverb and very similar in function to *subito* after **cum**. It can, for the same reason, be bracketed.

### clausos

Another secondary mediating marker between **quos** and some verb. But the **–os** is related by feedback to **quos** and consequently also to *oppidanos*, but not to *Coriolos* because *in* has intervened between *Coriolos* and *oppidanos*.

### habebat

Indicative verb, third person singular. This is, therefore, the closing marker to **quos**, whose accusative case is explained as denoting the recipient of the action of a verb: *habebat*. Thus the first nesting bracket

quos intus clausos habebat
is completed.

{**cum** [subito] exercitum [Romanum] Coriolos obsidentem **atque** [in oppidanos ⟨quos (intus) clausos habebat⟩ . . .

*intentum*

The *–um* marker resumes the thread after the bracket interruption and is, therefore, a secondary (mediating) marker. But also *–um* is associated by feedback with *exercitum* and with

Roman**um** Coriolos obsident**em atque in** oppidan**os**

It completes the incomplete idea expressed by

**in** oppidan**os**

giving

**in** oppidan**os** intent**um**.

Thus a unit can be made from *exercitum* to *intentum* including the completed bracket **quos** . . . . . . *habebat* and the bracket before **in** can now be removed because

In oppidan**os** intent**um**

is a single idea.

 {**cum** [subito] exercit**um** [Roman**um**] Coriol**os** obsident**em atque in** oppidan**os** [**quos** ⟨intus⟩ claus**os** hab**e**bat] intent**um** . . .

*sine*

Secondary marker indicating that the first opening marker **cum** has not yet been closed. It should also alert the reader to suspend judgement since there is insufficient evidence that *sine* is part of the ongoing sense from *intentum*. And as we have seen previously that prepositions can be the opening markers of small nesting units like *per forum* and *ad regem*, a tentative bracket [ could be opened.

*ullo*

*–o* is closing marker to *sine* but, as *ullo* is an epithet, it prepares the way for a noun as final closure; cf. {*regii*} *satellites* earlier.

*metu*

This *–u* was anticipated by the *–o* of *ullo* as closing marker to *sine*.

 {**cum** [subito] exercit**um** [Roman**um**] Coriol**os** obsident**em atque in** oppidan**os** [**quos** ⟨intus⟩ claus**os** hab**e**bat] intent**um** [**sine** ⟨ullo⟩ metu] . . .

*extrinsecus*

This does not close *sine*. It is an adverb and can thus be bracketed, as were *subito* and *intus*. It serves as a (mediating) reminder of the tentative brackets before *sine* and after *metu*.

*imminentis*

This is a secondary opening marker. *–is* shows genitive, which could by feedback be a definitive genitive to be taken with *metu*. But since it is an adjective it alerts the reader to expect a noun in the genitive case. It thus behaves as did *ullo* in anticipating *metu* and *regii* with *satellites*.

*belli*

*–i* denotes genitive singular and thus *belli* is the noun anticipated by *imminentis*. It completes another bracket. It also expands the idea of *intentum*.

> **in** oppidanos intentum [**sine** ⟨ullo⟩ metu ⟨extrinsecus⟩ ⟨**imminentis**⟩ belli]

This is a useful reminder of the importance of feedback.

*Volscae*

*–ae* indicates nominative feminine plural, or genitive feminine singular, or dative feminine singular. As there have been twenty words before it, the first possibility, i.e. that it is the delayed subject (see *regii satellites* in the previous sentence studied), seems likely. As an adjective it warns the translator to anticipate a noun, which will possibly have a more definite marker. It could, if nominative, be a mediating marker between *cum* and a verb not yet seen.

*legiones*

*–es* shows by feedback, that *–ae* is nominative, and also that it is mediating after *cum*.

> {**cum** [subito] exercitum [Romanum] Coriolos obsident**em atque in** oppidanos [quos ⟨intus⟩ clausos habe**bat** intentum [**sine** ⟨ullo⟩ metu ⟨extrinsecus⟩ imminent**is** belli] [Volscae] legion**es** . . .

*profectae*
–*ae* shows a connection by feedback with
> Volscae legiones . . .

It is a secondary marker after *legiones* and as an adjective can be bracketed; cf. *exercitum (Romanum)* and *(regii) satellites*.

**ab**
This is an opening marker of a bracket as with *per forum* (previous sentence) etc., and its secondary role is mediating since *(Volscae) legiones* has not been closed.

*Antio*
–*o* is the closing marker to **ab**, giving the small nesting bracket:

> ⟨ab Antio⟩
> {cum [subito] exercitum [Romanum] Coriolos obsidentem atque in oppidanos [quos ⟨intus⟩ clausos habebat] intentum [sine ⟨ullo⟩ metu ⟨extrinsecus⟩ ⟨imminentis⟩ belli] [Volscae] legiones [profectae ⟨ab Antio⟩] . . .

*invasissent*
After twenty-six words –**issent** provides the closing marker to the original **cum,** and the answer to the original question posed on p. 49: What closes **cum**? The answer, it now appears, is a subjunctive, not an ablative or indicative as were seen to be possibilities also from the learners' previous experience of **cum.** Thus we have a basic unit

> {cum . . . . . . exercitum . . . . . . legiones . . . . . . invasissent}

expanded by all the intervening units.

*eodemque*
This word constitutes a double marker. *eo–* denotes the ablative case and refers to the item-function of the adjective *eodem.* But –*que* is a co-ordinating marker resuming the **cum** and is equivalent to *atque.* (*que* after a word is the same as *et* or *atque* before it: *et Marcus, atque Marcus,*

*Marcusque.*) Indeed it is more; it is an opening marker since it stands instead of a second *cum* and prepares the mind of the reader for another, probably subjunctive, verb. Consequently, although one idea begun by *cum* has been completed, a second idea stemming from the same source is now begun, which will require a second verb in the subjunctive to complete, or close, it.

### tempore
*–ore* is ablative singular. It responds to, and closes, the item marker *eo–* of *eodemque*. It is a secondary marker stating that the opening marker *–que* has not been closed.

> . . . {[eodem] **que** [tempore]= {**atque cum** [eodem tempore]

### ex
This is an opening marker to another bracket, as *ab* was previously.

### oppido
*–o* is a closing marker to *ex*, giving the nesting bracket

> . . . [ex oppido]

### erupissent
*–issent* is the closing marker to *–que* equivalent to *cum.*

### hostes
*–es* is nominative or accusative plural. The first possibility is more likely because *–que* was closed without a subject expressed, because with some frequency *cum–* clause subjects stand outside their dependence marker parameters if the subject of the *cum* clause is the subject also of the main clause, and because the intransitive verb cannot govern an accusative. It acts, therefore, as a reinforcing closing marker to *erupissent.*

> . . . {[eodem] que [tempore] [ex oppido] erupissent hostess}

56

*forte*

This resumes the thread of the sentence after the bracket interruption. It is the fourth adverb in the sentence and like *subito*, *intus* and *extrinsecus* must be placed in a bracket. After all this time the mind, which has been dealing with numerous subordinate clauses and mediating markers, should be expecting the main clause, or elementary sentence.

**in**

This might well be a bracket opening marker, as were *ex*, *ab* and *in* previously.

*statione*

*–ione* closes *in*, to give yet another small nesting unit

    . . . [**in** stat**ione**]

*Marcus*

*–us* is nominative singular. The context now suggests that this word must be the subject of the elementary sentence. It is, therefore, an opening marker requiring a verb for its closure.

*fuit*

This is the closing marker to the nominative marker *–us* of *Marcus*. It serves by feedback to remind the reader that, just as the nominative *hostes* stood outside its parameters and that what was enclosed within the parameters did not form the full unit, so here,

    **in** stat**ione**

must constitute parts of the full expression

    **in** stat**ione** Marc**us fuit**

necessitating the removal of the bracket after *statione* to give one expression *in statione Marcus fuit*. In spite of the fact that no fewer than thirty-five words have gone before, it is these last four that give the basic, minimum information content of the sentence (Harris's 'elementary sentence').[1] The full sentence, as we have analysed it according to the marker information, can now be bracketed as follows:

[1]See above, page 31 and 34.

{Cum [subito] exercitum [Romanum] Coriolos obsidentem atque in oppidanos [quos ⟨intus⟩ clausos habebat] intentum [sine ⟨ullo⟩ metu ⟨extrinsecus⟩ imminentis belli] [Volscae] legiones [profectae ⟨ab Antio⟩] invasissent} {[eodem]que [tempore] [ex oppido] erupissent hostes} {forte} in statione Marcus fuit.[1]

In the strict application of string analysis all adjuncts (even such a small adjunct as the definite article) can be bracketed separately from their nouns. Similarly, both in English and Latin, all adjectives can be placed in brackets. Thus by applying such strict analysis to the present sentence it is possible to produce:

{cum [subito] exercitum [Romanum] [Coriolos obsidentem] [atque in oppidanos ⟨quos (intus) (clausos) habebat⟩ intentum] [⟨sine (ullo) metu (extrinsecus) (imminentis) belli⟩] [Volscae] legiones [profectae ⟨ab Antio⟩] invasissent} {[eodem] que [tempore] [ex oppido] erupissent hostes} {forte} in statione Marcus fuit

giving an elementary sentence

in statione Marcus fuit

expanded by two basic temporal units

cum exercitum legiones invasissent

and

cum erupissent hostes

both of which in turn are expanded by the bracketed adjuncts.

The above sentence is much more complex than anything seen so far. Yet there is a most significant point: nowhere in the whole of the analysis were we concerned with the English meaning of the Latin words, and, to emphasise this point, a translation was supplied only *after* the structural analysis. Instead we responded to the information content of the marker of each word—whether the marker was part of an individual item indicating no dependent unit, or a marker of dependence. To have looked for

[1]When suddenly the Volscian legions, having set out from Antium, had attacked the Roman army beseiging Colioli and concentrating, with no fear of an impending attack from without, on the townsfolk whom it held beseiged within, and when at the same time the enemy had made a sortie from the town, chance had it that Marcus was on sentry-go.

subjects, verbs and objects would have been the futile labour of Sisyphus. The markers of dependence provided the traffic lights permitting a safe passage through the ramifications of the sentence; they also gave contexts smaller than the total sentence that acted as parameters within which the item inflections could be assessed.

At the end of the analysis no 'sense' had been produced, where this is taken as the conventional production of a single English sentence, or a number of English sentences expressing the same idea as in the original Latin. But far more had been achieved, since the structure of the Latin sentence had been determined. Each word was assigned to a unit of speech clearly delineated by its opening and closing markers. Nothing could be removed from one context, violating its entirety, and assimilated to another context where it did not belong. As a result the chance of gross error arising when the reader attempted to convey in one or more English sentences the ideas contained in the Latin sentence—as is required by a more strict interpretation of translating—was greatly reduced, possibly eliminated altogether.

*

The type of complex sentence in the test battery which presented the least difficulty, and caused the least occurrence of gross error, had the following characteristics: the subject for the elementary sentence was clearly stated at the very beginning, to which the closing marker was clearly definable and situated at the very end of the sentence, and all subsidiary information nested between the beginning and the end of the elementary sentence. It was, consequently, a greatly expanded version of 'Marcus qui Romae habitat sapiens est' (p. 28). The subject's occurring early gave the translator something to hold on to as he plunged into the subordinate clauses, and increased his confidence in his ability to emerge safely on the other side. Such a sentence is given below. This is shown first as it would appear in a Latin text, and then with brackets and key markers added in bold type. It will also be observed that there is much greater similarity between the speech pattern of the Latin sentence and that of the English translation[1] than there was in the *cum subito* sentence:

> Celtiberi qui profecti erant domo deditionis ignari cum tandem superatis ubi primum imbres remiserunt amnibus Contrebiam venissent postquam nulla castra extra moenia viderunt aut in alteram partem translata rati aut recessisse hostes effusi per neglegentiam ad oppidum accesserunt.

> **celtiberi** {**qui** profecti **erant** [domo] [⟨deditionis⟩ ignari]} {**cum** [tandem] [super**atis** ⟨**ubi** primum imbres remis**erunt**⟩ amn**ibus**] Contrebiam ven**issent**} {**postquam** [⟨nulla⟩ castra ⟨extra moenia⟩] vid**erunt**} {**aut** ⟨**in** (alteram) partem⟩ translata] **rati** [**aut** recess**isse** hostes]} {effusi [**per** neglegentiam]} ad oppidum **accesserunt**

In a less exhaustive analysis (such as will be adopted later for the simple five-line—four-space stave) *domo* would be retained in the unit:

> qui profecti erant domo

The analysis given here is the strictest possible. For example, Harris would analyse *the man died*:

> man died—elementary sentence
> the      —adjunct to the left of *man*

whereas *the man died* could under less stringent analysis stand as the elementary sentence without removing the adjunct 'the' outside. In stave analysis the presentation of entire blocks needs to be emphasised, especially in the early stages.

From the above lengthy complex the basic information can be isolated in the elementary sentence:

> Celtiberi ad oppidum accesserunt
> The Celtiberi approached the town

In order to stress the extent of nesting within this elementary sentence—involving some thirty-four items subdivided into blocks or brackets as shown above—the whole of the first

---

[1]The Celtiberi, who had set out from home unaware of the surrender, when at length, having crossed the rivers as soon as the rains abated, they arrived at Contrebia, after they had seen no camp outside the wall, thinking either that it had been moved to another site, or that the enemy had withdrawn, they approached the town in disorderly array because of the carelessness which this induced.

and last words in the elementary sentence have been set in bold type. With strict adherence, however, to the interpretation of markers followed elsewhere in this text, only *–i* of *Celtiberi* and *–erunt* of *accesserunt* would be so stressed. Some non-clause markers, e.g. *in* of

     **in** alter**am** partem

together with the *–am* and *–em*, are also shown in bold type; for although they do not delineate the limits of major units or clauses, they provide secondary delineation, or assist by indicating small, bracketed, nesting units within the clause concerned but not integral parts of the simple clause proper.

*

In the final type of complex Latin sentence used in the research battery, the elementary sentence appears approximately half-way through the total complex. Thus the sentence consists of pre-elementary and post-elementary sentence expansion.[1] The example to illustrate this type of complex sentence follows, first in its normal textual presentation, then with the technique of bracketing applied:

> Postero die cum per exploratores cognovisset quo in loco hostes qui Brundisio profecti erant castra posuissent flumen transgressus est ut hostes extra moenia vagantes et nullis custodibus positis incautos ante solis occasum aggrederetur[2]

> {[poster**o**] di**e**} {**cum** [**per** exploratores] cogno**visset** [**quo in loco** hostes ⟨**qui** (Brundisio) profecti **erant**⟩ castra posu**issent**} flumen transgressus est {**ut** hostes [⟨extra moenia⟩ vagantes] [et ⟨(nul**lis**) custod**ibus posit**is⟩ incautos] [**ante** ⟨solis⟩ occas**um**] aggred**eretur**}

This sentence illustrates how unnecessary it is to attempt to isolate the main clause first. The translator, by initially ignoring

[1]As Harris would describe it, 'of adjuncts to the left and right of the elementary sentence'.

[2]On the following day when he had ascertained through scouts where the enemy, who had set out from Brundisium, had pitched camp, he crossed the river in order to attack before sunset the enemy wandering off guard outside the defence walls with no sentries posted. This sentence first appeared on p. 34.

61

clauses preceding the main clause, can attach insufficient importance to them. And because these clauses are often more clearly delineated than the main clause itself, evaluating them has—by reductive analysis—the effect of leaving the main clause isolated as required. Far less to-and-fro eye movement is required in following this approach than in the haphazard search for the main clause before any of the subordinate expanding units are defined. The translator who responds to the marker of each Latin word in its natural sentence order, as he does with his mother tongue, learns more about word order in Latin than he would by any method seeking to impart understanding only by altering the word order. This view was advanced in Chapter Two when the technique of suspending judgement was discussed.

There is a basic similarity between the techniques of bracketing described above and that of string analysis employed by Harris: both uncover the main or elementary sentence by setting aside strings of words that are not the elementary sentence, and whose removal still leaves a well-formed sentence. While the method described by Harris is unlikely to correspond to the sequence of events taking place in speaking or listening, it does have two relevant features. First, it brings out clearly dependence relations of any order; second, and more important, it illustrates efficiently the nesting structure of the language. The significance of an application of this for translating from Latin into English has been discussed in this chapter.

The completed analysis may be expressed as a rule:

Every opening bracket '(' is closed by the closing marker ')' $n+1$ to its right, where $n$ is the number of opening brackets intervening between itself and this closing bracket.

This corresponds to three rules governing the psychological behaviour of speakers and writers:

(a) A dependent string, once entered, must be completed before re-entering the kernel string.

(b) A second-order dependency, once entered, must be completed before the original first-order dependent string is re-entered.

(c) The process may be iterated to $n$th-order dependencies.

In English, usage restricts the number and length of such hierarchical nestings. Latin may have similar limitations, but the limits are considerably wider. The limits in Latin verse are considerably wider (on occasions) than those in prose, the narrow limits in the latter greatly reducing the cognitive strain on speaker or writer and likewise on hearer or reader.

From the point of view of the hearer or reader, the decoding of messages is further aided by linguistic markers, such as commas or pauses or changes in inflection. But linguistic markers may also take the form of words or parts of words and it is these that are so important in reading, or translating, Latin. Whatever their form, their syntactic function is always the same: to signal the entries to and exits from dependence strings, or, as in

not only . . . but also . . .

the approach of the second kernel string, and its arrival. The syntactic function of markers is quite distinct from their semantic function.

The linguistic and applied techniques discussed above constitute the basis of stave analysis, to be discussed in the next chapter. But the technique of bracketing, while clear to the experienced language student and linguistically sound in itself, suffers from two shortcomings. These concern the teaching of pupils beginning a study of Latin and, more fundamentally, the reforming of the translation habits of fourth and fifth formers taught by outmoded methods. The first drawback is that the bracketing of a sentence, particularly for younger pupils, is a complicated process and may confuse rather than clarify. The second, and more important, is that, although the bracketing technique isolates all the clauses and sets their limits, and shows the elementary sentence as an entity, it does nothing to uncover the hierarchical structure of the sentences. Even if different bracket shapes are used as in this chapter, the words still appear in conventional lines of print and the different types of brackets place an additional perceptual and cognitive strain on the young learner. Moreover the eye movement required to check where the opening { or [ or 〈 was in the sentence when the closing } or ] or 〉 has been determined, is very considerable. Analyses of the three sentences considered in this chapter illustrates this point. In physical terms the sentences have different shapes. The shape is not apparent via the brackets. Consequently while the bracketing method teaches something that is necessary to a full understanding of word order, it does not do so with all possible clarity. And in the full Latin course based on the stave the fundamental technique would be introduced much earlier, to children whose linguistic knowledge and experience are more limited.

The physical shape of sentences is important since one cannot expect to find the elementary sentence always in the same position in relation to the adjuncts. This was highlighted earlier in an example in which children translated *Bruto*, the first word in the sentence, as nominative because it stood in a position frequently occupied by the subject in English.[1]

Among the markers possible in language are voice inflections, and every language has melody and cadence—readily appreciated by the trained ear of those skilled in the use of a given language. But the beginner in Latin does not yet possess such skill, and to acquire it needs every possible assistance. This could include, at the appropriate stages, an appeal to the eye as well as the ear. The diagrams below show graphically our three complex sentence types as presented orally and received aurally, where the rising and falling of the curve represents voice cadence:

(a) Sentence beginning *Cum subito exercitum* . . .

(b) Sentence beginning *Celtiberi qui profecti erant* . . .

(c) Sentence beginning *Postero die cum* . . .

[1]See above, p. 40.

The curves reveal how conventional lines of print are of little use for showing the syntactical hierarchy of a Latin sentence. Only the time taken to complete an utterance can be represented in conventional print. Yet meaningful utterances do not proceed in straight lines but as indicated by the curves above. While skilful reading of the sentence by the teacher will assist in the understanding of rhythm and cadence, the inexperienced translator cannot rely for long on the evidence of his ear. Long before he reaches the end of a complex sentence the information, derived from the melody etc. presented to his ear, will have vanished; only the evidence continuing before his eyes throughout his translation will sustain him to the very end.

Stave analysis was, therefore, designed with the object of throwing light on the hierarchical structure of the Latin sentence. Its purpose was to show the bracketing technique in clearer relief; to reveal the elementary sentence unmistakeably to the eye by a means other than that of conventional print; to show the relationship of every other component unit to the elementary sentence and to each other by their relative positions; and to reduce to a minimum the random to-and-fro eye movement in the translator or reader. The result is an analysis on a stave by which each sentence is seen to possess a physical shape peculiar to itself determined by its syntactical structure.

*Chapter Four*

## STAVE ANALYSIS

### THE PRINCIPLES OF THE METHOD

STAVE ANALYSIS seeks to make clear to the inexperienced translator the bracketing principle discussed in the last chapter. The *blocks* it uses, representing the complete units of speech that together constitute the syntactical hierarchy of the complex sentence, are identifiable with brackets, themselves identifiable in principle with Harris's strings. It is, therefore, in effect, a type of string analysis of a Latin sentence.

It is possible to make the blocks of stave analysis precisely the same in size and content as Harris's strings, which was done in the case of the brackets. However, this would impose two limitations on the stave analysis method:

(i) Staves with different numbers of spaces would be required for sentences of different complexities, as will be illustrated.

(ii) By carrying out an analysis as precise as that required to produce exact strings, it is possible, especially in the early stages of the use of stave analysis, to obscure the totality of the component blocks.[1]

It was felt that a deeper impression would be made on the learner if, from the outset, he saw the different physical shapes of different sentences always on a five line—four-space stave, and if he saw the blocks as total entities. A simple example will illustrate the second point. In the sentence:

[1]Haas in *Linguistic Relevance* (p. 14) writes: An utterance may be segmented in an infinite number of ways, and, theoretically, the segments may be of any size. What is linguistically relevant is not this physical operation of cutting, but the decision *where* to make the cuts.

rati sunt castra in alteram partem translata esse

they though that the camp had been moved to another site
the translator is principally concerned with two units of speech:
a main block representing the elementary sentence:

rati sunt

and a second block directly dependent on it:

castra in alteram partem translata esse

These two blocks would be placed on the five-line—four-space stave as follows:

| | rati sunt | | |
|---|---|---|---|
| | | castra in alteram partem translata esse | |
| | | | |
| | | | |

The enclosing of the blocks by vertical and horizontal lines is a schematic indication that the content of any block is inviolable. This is represented linguistically by the markers of dependence, which reinforce the schematic representation of the lines by appearing in bold type. Strictly speaking the parameter markers of the dependent block are the *–a* of *castra* and the *–a esse* of *translata esse* However, in the initial stages, greater visual emphasis is produced if the whole words are printed in bold type.

Because the second block is subordinate to the first it does not possess linguistic parity of status with the first block; thus it is assigned a lower place on the stave. Because it is a first-order dependency, i.e. directly dependent on the main block, it appears *one* space below the main block and its first word begins immediately after the last word of the block on which it directly depends. This applies to all blocks that are first order dependencies, whether they depend directly on the main block, or directly on a block which is itself subordinate to the main block, provided that, in the Latin sentence, it follows the block on which it depends. Thus in the sentence:

exploratores praemisit qui cognoscerent quo in loco hostes essent

he sent scouts forward to discover the whereabouts of the enemy

67

the stave analysis would be:

| exploratores praemisit | | | |
|---|---|---|---|
| | qui cognoscerent | | |
| | | quo in loco hostes essent | |
| | | | |

The translator is shown that it is both physically and syntactically impossible for the block

> **quo in loco** hostes **essent**

to be taken as directly dependent on the main block

> exploratores praemisit

Yet it is precisely this sort of error which was found in the research to be responsible for gross error. It is equivalent to making the *bus* rather than the *man* wear *an overcoat*.[1]

The second feature of this approach is that, when the complex sentence is presented on the stave, the original Latin word and clause order is maintained. Clauses may be moved vertically to denote their precise degree of dependence and the clauses on which they depend. They may not at any time or under any circumstances be transposed horizontally. Thus if the order of the sentence analysed above were presented as:

> exploratores qui quo in loco hostes essent cognoscerent praemisit

which is improbable owing to the ugliness of the three consecutive verbs, the degree of dependence would be shown in exactly the same way as in the first illustration, i.e. by vertical, not by horizontal, stave movement. The new presentation would be:

| exploratores | | | | praemisit |
|---|---|---|---|---|
| | qui | | cognoscerent | |
| | | quo in loco hostes essent | | |
| | | | | |

[1]See above, page 31 and 32.

68

Thus the clause directly dependent on another clause still appears in the space below the clause on which it depends, but no longer in such a way that its first word begins immediately after the last word of the other clause. To bring that circumstance about would require a forbidden alteration of the original word order. Instead, the dependent clause appears in the space below the clause on which it depends directly but immediately below the gap left by its own removal. This will apply to all nesting units of dependence.

The point has already been made that there can be degrees of precision in the analysis, and staves of different numbers of lines to accommodate such variation in degree. While the sentence:

rati sunt castra in alteram partem translata esse

was clearly presented as two blocks on the four-space stave:

| rati sunt | | |
|---|---|---|
| | castra in alteram partem translata esse | |

a strict application of string analysis would require:

| rati sunt | | | | | |
|---|---|---|---|---|---|
| | castra | | | translata esse | |
| | | in | | partem | |
| | | | alteram | | |

This second analysis, while more correct in terms of string analysis technique, does not give so clear an idea of the total entity of a second block directly dependent on a first. An idea can be gained of how many stave spaces would be required for the sentences analysed in the last chapter if we add two words to the above sentence and see that this addition requires a fifth stave space:

quia rati sunt castra in alteram partem translata esse abierunt
because they thought that the camp had been moved to another site they went away

This would appear in the following form:

69

| | | | | | abierunt | |
|---|---|---|---|---|---|---|
| quia rati sunt | | | | | | |
| | castra | | | translata esse | | |
| | | in | partem | | | |
| | | alteram | | | | |

At this point another advantage of analysis by the stave emerges. In the bracket presentation sometimes a word that is a marker denoting the end of a bracket, and as such not removable from the bracket, has to be removed in order to show that another string of words in another bracket is dependent on it. For example, if brackets are applied to the sentences:

> **ut** per exploratores cogno**scerent quo in loco** hostes **essent**

> to find out through scouts where the enemy were

we would have:

> {**ut** [per exploratores] cogno**scerent**}
> {**quo in loco** hostes **essent**}

requiring cogno**scerent** to be at one and the same time inside the top inviolable bracket, and also outside it, because the bracket

> {**quo in loco** hostes **essent**}

depends directly on it. This idea is clearly presented schematically on the stave through the combination of vertical and horizontal lines with the linguistic representation of dependence markers in bold type and by the respective stave placings of the blocks; together these indicate that the units are inviolable and show subordinate position of the dependent unit.

Another weakness of the bracket method noted in the last chapter is that the elementary-sentence bracket is not shown in a prominent position. In the string analysis discussed in Chapter Two the elementary sentence *man caught bus* was placed at the top of the list of adjuncts, or strings.[1] For physical shapes reflecting the melodies and cadences of the hierarchical structures of complex sentences to be effective, the elementary

[1]See page 31.

sentence must stand out clearly from what the bracket process reveals to come before and/or after, or inside, it. This did not happen, however, on bracketing the three complex sentences in the last chapter. In the first, the elementary sentence came right at the end after many cadences; in the second, all dependencies nested within the elementary sentence, which appeared partly at the very beginning of the complex and partly at the very end; and in the third, the elementary sentence appeared approximately half-way through the complex. In none of the three bracketed complexes would the elementary sentence have been quickly obvious to anyone other than an expert analyser.

This difficulty is overcome through stave analysis; the elementary sentence is always given the same vertical position, being placed in the top stave space, though it is not always in the same horizontal situation within that space. This will become apparent on looking at the three complex sentences bracketed in Chapter Three that are now re-presented on the staves below. As we should expect, the horizontal location of the elementary sentence is very different in the three instances; this reflects the very different cadence graphs shown on page 64. The sentences are each given four times in accordance with the various analyses previously described. These are:
(i) as they would appear in a standard textbook presented in conventional lines of print
(ii) bracketed and with key markers shown in bold type
(iii) after analysis on the stave in the basic form stressing the totality of units
(iv) after strict analysis on the stave conforming to the bracketing and Harris's strings.
A translation is provided as a fifth presentation.

A.  cum subito exercitum Romanum Coriolos obsidentem atque in oppidanos quos intus clausos habebat intentum sine ullo metu extrinsecus imminentis belli Volscae legiones profectae ab Antio invasissent eodemque tempore ex oppido erupissent hostes forte in statione Marcus fuit.

B.  {Cum [subito] exercitum [Romanum] [Coriolos obsidentem] [atque in oppidanos ⟨**quos** (intus) (clausos) hab**ebat**⟩

intentum] [⟨sine (ullo) metu (extrinsecus) (imminentis) belli⟩] [Volscae] legiones [profectae ⟨ab Antio⟩] invas**issent**} {[eo**dem**] **que** [tempore] [ex oppido] erup**issent hostes**} {forte} in statione Marcus **fuit.**}

C. ⎫
   ⎬ See insert between pages 72–73.
D. ⎭

E.   When suddenly the Volscian legions, having set out from Antium, had attacked the Roman army besieging Corioli and concentrating, with no fear of an impending attack from without, on the townsfolk whom it held besieged within, and when at the same time the enemy had made a sortie from the town, chance had it that Marcus was on sentry-go.

F.   Celtiberi qui profecti erant domo deditionis ignari cum tandem superatis ubi primum imbres remiserunt amnibus Contrebiam venissent postquam nulla castra extra moenia viderunt[1] aut in alteram partem translata rati aut recessisse hostes effusi per neglegentiam ad oppidum accesserunt.

G.   Celtiberi {**qui profecti erant** [domo] [⟨deditionis⟩ ignari]} {**cum** [tandem] [super**atis** ⟨**ubi primum** imbres remis**erunt**⟩ amn**ibus**] Contrebiam ven**issent**} {**postquam** [⟨nulla⟩ castra ⟨extra moenia⟩] vid**erunt**} {[aut ⟨**in** (alteram) partem⟩ translata] **rati** ]aut recess**isse** host**es**]} [2] {effusi [per neglegentiam]} ad oppidum access**erunt**

[1] {*Postquam nulla castra extra moenia viderunt*} —
        after they saw that there was no camp outside the walls.
N.B. Livy here uses an elliptical statement omitting the infinitive *esse*. Normal usage would be:
    *Postquam viderunt nulla castra esse*—after they saw that there was no camp.

[2] {[Aut in alteram partem translata] rati [aut recessisse hostes]} The *aut* . . . . . . *aut* . . . . . . gives two more accusatives and infinitives both depending on *rati* Again *esse* is omitted in the first one:
        rati castra in alteram partem translata esse
thinking that the camp had been moved to another site
Although Livy says that they thought, *after* they saw that no camp was outside the walls (postquam viderunt nulla castra extra moenia), that one of two events had happened, they really made the deduction *because* they saw no camp. No camp meant either that the enemy had moved it elsewhere, or that they had gone away entirely.

H. ⎫
       ⎬  See insert between pages 72–73.
I. ⎭

J.   The Celtiberi, who had set out from home unaware of the
     surrender, when at last, after crossing the rivers as soon as
     the rains abated, they arrived at Contrebia, after they saw
     that there was no camp outside the walls, thinking either
     that it had been moved to another site or that the enemy
     had withdrawn, they approached the town in disorderly
     array because of the carelessness which this induced.

K.   postero die cum per exploratores cognovisset quo in loco
     hostes qui Brundisio profecti erant castra posuissent
     flumen transgressus est ut hostes extra moenia vagantes et
     nullis custodibus positis incautos ante solis occasum
     aggrederetur.

L.   ({[postero] die} {cum [per exploratores] cognovisset
     [quo in loco hostes ⟨qui (Brundisio) profecti erant⟩
     castra posuissent]} flumen transgressus est {ut hostes
     [⟨extra moenia⟩ vagantes] [et ⟨(nullis) custodibus positis⟩
     incautos] [ante ⟨solis⟩ occasum] aggrederetur})

M. ⎫
       ⎬  See insert between pages 72–73.
N. ⎭

O.   On the next day, when he had found out through scouts
     where the enemy, who had set out from Brundisium, had
     pitched camp, he crossed the river in order to make an
     attack before nightfall on the enemy who were wandering
     carelessly, without sentries posted, outside the defence
     walls.

Enclosing the blocks within vertical and horizontal lines gives
visual perception of linguistic inviolability and facilitates the
teaching of the idea that sentences even as complex as these are
no more than simple sentences greatly expanded by the addition

73

of smaller units. Just as the elementary sentence may be expanded by the addition of blocks before or after it, or by the insertion of nesting blocks within it, so its simple information content can be isolated by the removal in toto of all dependent blocks. The removal of a single block in toto does not violate the elementary sentence, or alter its basic information content. The removal of one block reduces by one unit the total information content of the syntactical complex, while further removal of blocks will eventually reduce this total information content unit by unit until the basic information content of the elementary sentence is laid bare.

The stave provides the translator with a number of clearly defined contexts, each of which is smaller than the total complex sentence. The parameters of each of these smaller contexts are the markers of dependence and these are clearly shown in bold type. Once each block has been isolated and placed in its appropriate stave position, the translator is confronted by a number of units of speech each of which in itself is as simple as anything met in the early stages of the Latin course. The most complex sentence breaks down into blocks, which often prove to be of surprising simplicity once they have been defined. After the parameters have been determined, attention can be turned to the interaction within the block of the constituent item markers.

When both item and dependence markers have been evaluated, the structural meaning of the complex sentence has been determined. The translator is then at liberty to refer to the dictionary to discover the meanings of any words unknown to him. But such dictionary use is the last link in the chain, not the first.

Finally it must be observed that stave analysis is a teaching method not merely a visual aid. In the early stages the pupil will be presented with sentences analysed for him. But the ultimate aim of the method is that the process of analysis will become internalised, and that the pupil will carry out the analysis for himself, first consciously and deliberately by making his own stave, finally unconsciously and automatically by responding to the markers in the way in which a skilled reader of Latin responds.

Success is achieved with a teaching method when pupils acquire an understanding of the techniques being taught them and are able to apply them on their own. For the teacher to produce this result he must satisfy two basic requirements. First, he must have a method to offer—and unfortunately, in the matter of Latin translation, some teachers have no specific method to offer. Secondly, the method must be sufficiently clearly explained and sound in essence for the pupil not only to understand it but to be able to apply it for himself.

If stave analysis is introduced at the earliest stage possible, the sentence concerned need be no more complex than

      Marcus bonum amicum habet

      Marcus has a good friend

analysed as:

| | Marcus | | amicum habet | |
|---|---|---|---|---|
| | | bonum | | |

By the time sentences of the complexity analysed in this text are encountered, the pupil will either be able to make his own visual aid[1]—perhaps with occasional assistance from the Latin teacher—or will be able to dispense with the visual aid altogether because he has learnt to perform the process of analysis automatically as his eye travels along a line of conventional print. If this is so, he will be virtually in the position of being able to read Latin rather than translate it. At present too few pupils in the Latin course are able to do this. Consequently many of those who begin the study of the Latin language and drop it after the 'O' level examination of the G.C.E. never progress to reading Latin literature. By presenting the reading processes right from the first stages of the Latin course, stave analysis aims to accelerate the acquisition of reading ability and to make this skill available long before the Sixth Form is reached, and to more than a mere handful of students of Latin.

[1]See Appendix 3: Stave presentation of textual examples.

*Chapter Five*

# GRAMMAR AND LINGUISTICS

### THEIR IMPLICATION FOR LATIN TEACHING

WE HAVE FREQUENTLY heard it said that the term *linguistics* is merely a euphemism for *grammar* and that behind a facade of modernity there lurks something of great age. Critics voicing such a view continue by saying that linguistics differs from grammar principally in giving new technical terms to parts of the language that grammar had traditionally known by other definitive terms. Unless some distinction is drawn between the grammatical and linguistic approaches there is likely to be little progress made among the sceptics.

In its widest sense linguistics is the study of *language* as distinct from the study of a language. It is consequently a study of the verbal behaviour of mankind, and seeks to find common elements in such behaviour so that generalisations may be drawn from numerous acts of verbal behaviour. From the study, verbal behavioural acts possessing certain clearly defined characteristics can be grouped and classified according to type. The grammarian and the linguist both use the term *rule* for these groupings or generalisations. But the linguist regards rules as *summaries of behaviour*, which are consequently primarily *descriptive* of verbal behaviour and function only secondarily as *prescriptive* as with the old use of Latin grammar.[1]

The linguist is also concerned primarily with the classification of total utterances; he is less concerned with such details as inflections, which enabled the old grammarian to classify individual items in declensions and conjugations. Fries gives

[1]See in this respect Politzer, *Teaching French : An Introduction to Applied Linguistics*, p. 11.

76

the following account of the difference between grammar and linguistics:

> We would then define linguistics or linguistic science as a body of knowledge and understanding concerning the nature and functioning of human language, built up out of information about the structure, the operation and the history of a wide range of very diverse human languages by means of those techniques and procedures that have proved most successful in establishing verifiable generalisations concerning relationships among linguistic phenomena.[1]

He says elsewhere:

> In other words, the traditional grammar starts from the meanings, which are assumed to be intuitive responses to the whole string of words as lexical items, and requires that the particular words and groups of words to which these meanings are applied be assigned certain technical names.[2] The whole process seems to be one of analysis of the meanings for the sake of assigning certain technical names to particular words or groups of words.

> Our structural approach to grammar differs fundamentally in purpose and assumptions from that of the traditional school grammar. It recognises all the grammatical meanings of the traditional grammar, but does not accept either of the assumptions (a) that the recognition of these meanings are intuitive responses, or (b) that they arise out of the fusion of the meanings of separate words. This structural approach assumes that whatever grammatical meanings there are, are definitely conveyed by signals; that these signals consist of structures, identified by contrastive patterns of functioning structural units; and that these units can be described in terms of the contrastive arrangements and forms of these functional units.[3]

Chomsky, putting the case for generative linguistics which produces generative grammars, says:

[1]*Linguistics and Reading*, p. 91.
[2]Condemned as 'belonging to a pre-scientific era' by Fries in *The Structure of English* (see bibliography).
[3]*Linguistics and Reading*, p. 71.

The fundamental aim in the linguistic analysis of a language L is to separate the grammatical sequences of L from the ungrammatical sequences which are not sentences of L and to study the structure of the grammatical sequences. The grammar of L will thus be a device which generates all the grammatical sequences of L and none of the ungrammatical ones . . .

A generative grammar, in the sense of syntactic structures, is not a large collection of neatly organised examples and hints as to how to construct similar ones . . .

A generative grammar is a system of explicit rules that assigns to each sequence of phones, whether of the observed corpus or not, a structural description that contains all the information about how this sequence of phones is represented on each of several linguistic levels[1]—in particular, information as to whether this sequence of phones is a properly formed or grammatical sentence, and if not in what respects it deviates from well-formedness. The study of generative grammar is, however, a natural outgrowth of traditional descriptive linguistics. Modern linguistics has, typically, been concerned with much narrower problems of constructing several inventories of elements in terms of which utterances can be represented, and has given little attention to the rules that generate utterances with structural descriptions.[2]

Several points raised in the two passages above have been a recurring theme throughout this text. The first is the concern with structure rather than with items; this is an area in which linguistics can be seen to differ considerably from grammar. Haas puts the point very cogently:

To try to account for the many and various meaningful utterances in terms of 'recurrent elements in recurrent relations' is not to set ourselves two tasks—(i) to find the elements, and (ii) to establish the relations. We cannot do the one without the other. This is why linguistic theory is a theory of linguistic *structure*, and modern linguistics is

---

[1]The linguist can be concerned with morphemic and phonemic levels of language (see Haas, *Linguistic Relevance*, p. 23 et alibi).
[2]Cited apud Fries: *Linguistics and Reading*, pp. 88–89.

known as 'structural linguistics.' What is essential about linguistic elements (and more important than their intrinsic properties) is the fact that they are terms in a systematic network of mutual relations, terms in a structure.[1]

It is precisely this that stave analysis attempts to emphasise and that makes it differ fundamentally from many of the approaches used in the translation of complex Latin sentences.

The second point, made by Fries, is that many conventional grammar lessons both in English and in Latin consist of little more than assigning technical definitions to parts and units of speech. Thus in Latin a student may be able to 'name the ablative absolute'. He may also be able to define it as a 'noun in the ablative case together with a present or past participle in the same case'. In English he may be able to assign to a certain string of words the definition 'adjectival clause describing the noun *man*'. He may also be capable of a high level of linguistic competence, demonstrated regularly by his uttering, and even writing, sentences in his mother tongue that deviate considerably from the rules of generative grammar relating to well-formedness. But while such a student can define the ablative absolute and may be able to recognise it when in a form that coincides precisely with his definition because the two components are adjacent, as in the sentence:

urbe capta cives necaverunt
when the city had been taken they killed the citizens

he may be completely unable to recognise the construction when the component elements are separated, as in the sentence:

cum tandem superatis ubi primum imbres remiserunt amnibus Contrebiam venissent
when at length, after they had forded the river as soon as the rains abated, they reached Contrebia

Nowhere is the existence of this phenomenon more clearly indicated than in the severe decline in marks obtained by students as the course procedes—and the marks are used to assess ability in Latin. This decline is not accidental.

In the early stages the pupil receives most of his marks for his ability to reproduce, either orally or in writing, declensions, conjugations or vocabulary lists which he has committed to

[1]*Linguistic Relevance*, page 8.

memory by rote. Such translation as is attempted is of simple sentences consisting of a minimum number of rote-learned items, and often undertaken immediately after the rote learning has taken place. It is a simple process of using the building stones of Politzer to produce the bridge of communication.[1]

Later the connection between grammar and translation becomes more tenuous because it is less directly related. In the second year the pupil is required to learn 'grammatical constructions'. A favourite method of testing the degree of success in this field is to require him to translate English sentences into Latin. For example, following the learning of rules for purpose clauses, sentences will take the form of:

We crossed the river in order to reach the other bank

He is coming in order to see his friend

The men went to the games to see the charioteer

or may show clauses in reverse order within the sentence:

In order not to be seen he concealed himself in a bush

In order to reach Rome early he hastened his steps

These sentences illustrate the structure of the 'examples' used to demonstrate the 'rule' that 'in clauses expressing purpose, *ut* or *ne* is followed by the present subjunctive if the main verb is primary, and by the imperfect subjunctive if the main verb is historic'.

There are still two dangers in translating from English apart from accepting a rule of grammar as being *prescriptive*, which makes the nature and function of the rule similar to that of a formula in physics—something to be applied in solving a specific and clearly worded problem. The first is that the English sentence differs little in complexity from the most elementary form of complex sentence seen by the learner in the first few months of the Latin course; it resembles the simple presentation of the ablative absolute in the first of the illustrative sentences above. Second, the form of the English sentence reinforces the malpractice of 'translating' each item as it comes without relating it to the total structure, or of hopping about from one word to another, e.g. from main verb direct to subordinate verb. If each word is translated as it is met, translation from English into Latin becomes a process of one-to-one

[1]See above, page 17.

relationships, of substituting one item for another semantically equivalent item.

Many Latin learners do think, however, that translation consists precisely in finding equivalent lexical meanings in a dictionary, working at the item instead of at the structural level. And once the way grammar is learned ceases to be reflected directly in techniques used for translation from Latin into English, and once the rote-learned grammar and its reproduction ceases to play so great a part in pupil assessment, marks for performance decline, sometimes alarmingly.

This type of approach has its parallel in certain examination questions. It is not uncommon for an 'O' level translation piece to be followed by 'syntax questions'. These are of the following kind:

Account for the mood and tense of *aggrederetur* and for the case of *multo* in translation piece 1.

These questions are merely stimuli evoking a response that is no more than the reproduction of a rote-learned rule. Thus the answer to the question will be:

*aggrederetur* is imperfect subjunctive: subjunctive because it is the subordinate verb in a purpose clause; imperfect because the main verb is historic. *multo* is an ablative of measure of difference.

Such learning persists even at higher levels in Latin courses. Not many years ago one examining body, in the report by its examiners on defects in the answers of candidates entered for 'A' level[1] Latin, complained that too many candidates when asked to explain 'irregularities of syntax' gave answers such as: 'Cicero here breaks the rule for purpose clauses'. It is a sad reflection on teaching methods when learners of seventeen and eighteen years of age, who have been studying Latin for five or six years, make such statements.

Yet no attempt is made to solve the problem by introducing improved teaching approaches, and the prescriptive rule and the item-by-item translation techniques are perpetuated. Combined with these, or more strictly as a result of these, come descriptions of translation methods as producing in pupils the ability to 'see their way through a sentence', an expression which on analysis

[1]General Certificate of Education, Advanced Level.

turns out to be so nebulous as to be meaningless; or such pieces of advice as to 'isolate the main clause first'. As has already been argued, both these objectives are dangerous rules of thumb. The danger is made plain by Garvin and Reifler when describing machine translation:

> A translation programme, to be useful, has to accomplish more than merely one by one transfer of units from the source language to the target language. It has to include some solution to the problems of choice implicit in the fact that (a) a unit in the source language may have more than one equivalent in the target language, and (b) that the order of source language units may not be suitable for output in the target language . . . The required selection can only be programmed if the contextual conditions can be determined under which any given decision from several possible ones is to be implemented. The linguist's major contribution to machine translation is the discovery of these conditions and in the formulation of a routine for basing decisions on it.[1]

It is evident from the observations of Fries and Chomsky quoted in this chapter that linguistics does not require the abandonment of *all* that grammar has said in the past; but it is equally evident that there needs to be a good deal of reappraisal, and quite possibly some abandonment.

Fries goes on to say that:

> The findings of science in language, as in other spheres of life, frequently necessitate the abandoning of many long, and often fondly held (pre-scientific) ideas. Accordingly the linguist, because he has acquired an extensive corpus of knowledge about language, is forced to abandon many of the views of the grammars and dictionaries of the latter half of the eighteenth century together with the grammars and dictionaries themselves as no longer adequate to explain the nature and function of language.[2]

It is not surprising that this is especially applicable to Latin, which continues to be taught largely in the most traditional and conservative of ways.

[1]Cited apud Fries, *Linguistics and Reading*, p. 84.
[2]*Linguistics and Reading*, p. 67.

# BIBLIOGRAPHY

Incorporated Association of Assistant Masters in Secondary Schools: *The Teaching of Classics*, Cambridge University Press, 1954

Ursula Bellugi and Roger Brown: *The Acquisition of Language*—Monographs of the Society for Research in Child Development, Serial No. 92, Vol. 29, No. 1. (The Antioch Press, Yellow Springs, Ohio, 1964)

Noam Chomsky: *Syntactic Structures* (Mouton & Co., The Hague, 1957). 'Some Methodological Remarks on Generative Grammar', Word, (18 August, 1961) 221–223

Charles C. Fries: *The Structure of English: An Introduction to the Construction of English Sentences* (Harcourt, Brace and World Inc., New York, 1952); (Longmans, Green & Co., London, 1957)
*Linguistics and Reading* (Holt, Rinehart and Winston Inc., New York, 1962)

Paul Garvin and Erwin Reifler: *Proceedings of the Eighth International Congress on Linguistics* (Oslo University Press, 1958)

William Haas: 'Linguistic Relevance'—one of a collection of essays in a commemorative volume *In Memory of J. R. Firth* (Longmans Green & Co., London, 1966)

Zellig S. Harris: *String Analysis of Sentence Structure* (Mouton & Co., The Hague, 1961)

Robert Lado: *Language Teaching: A Scientific Approach* (McGraw Hill Inc., New York, 1964)

Robert L. Politzer: *Teaching French: An Introduction to Applied Linguistics* (Blaisdell Publishing Co., 1965)

Sol Saporta: *Psycholinguistics: A Book of Readings* (Holt, Rinehart and Winston Inc., New York, 1961)

*Appendix* 1 (*a*)

## CLASSIFICATION OF MARKERS

It has been shown throughout this text that there are different types of markers which perform different linguistic functions. Markers can be classified as follows:

1. BY WORD STRUCTURE
   a. *Whole-word markers* are those where the whole word acts as a marker (e.g. conjunctions, adverbs, prepositions)
   b. *Inflection markers* are those formed by the change of only part of the word through declining or conjugating that word (e.g. the –a, –a, –am, –ae, –ae and –a in:
      mensa
      mensa
      mens**am**
      mens**ae**
      mens**ae**
      mensa
   and the –o, –as, –at, –amus, –atis and –ant in:
      am**o**
      am**as**
      am**at**
      am**amus**
      am**atis**
      am**ant**

2. BY CATEGORY
   a. *An item marker* is any single-word marker that stands on its own. All markers are in fact item markers.
   b. *A co-ordinating marker* is a conjunction (see whole-word markers in 1*a*) and may link two items as in *Marcus et Sextus*, or two elementary sentences as in *Romam iit et*

84

*amicum vidit*, or two dependent units as in *qui Romam iit et amicum vidit*.

  c. *Dependence markers* (*or markers of dependence*) are those which 'open' and 'close' a dependent unit in a complex sentence. Acting in combination they mark the limits and chief characteristics of the dependent unit, as in *Romam iit **ut amicum suum videret***.

  It will be seen that dependence markers are generally a combination of 1*a* and 1*b* above.

3. BY FUNCTION
  These [with the exception of co-ordinating markers (2*b* above)] can be:

  a. *Opening* if they open (or begin) an elementary sentence unit or dependent unit of speech.
  b. *Secondary* (or mediating) if they function between the opening marker (*a* above) and closing marker (*c* below) to indicate that the unit of speech has been opened but that a closing marker has not yet been seen.
  c. *Closing* if they close the elementary sentence unit or dependent unit of speech. The following example shows a dependent unit containing an opening marker, closing marker and two secondary or mediating markers:

    **ut** amic**um** su**um** vid**eret**

  Opening and secondary (or mediating) markers are said to be *prospective*, as they anticipate a closing marker, they require the reader to *suspend judgement* until the closing marker is found.

  Closing markers are said to be *retrospective*, as they operate by *feedback* on the previous markers to yield the complete meaning of the elementary sentence or dependent unit.

  Subordinate phrases may have opening, closing and secondary (mediating) markers, but are not considered to be defined by markers of dependence; e.g. **in** urb**e**, **in** magna urb**e**.

*Appendix* ı (*b*)

## TABLE OF MARKER TYPES

*Bruto*
Strict item marker. It tells us something about him which differs from the *–us* in *Brutus*.

*Brutus and Bruto*
Both inflection markers caused by declining the noun.

*Bruto obviam ivit*
The *–o* here is an opening marker.

*Iuveni Bruto obviam ivit*
The *–o* of *Bruto* is a secondary (mediating) marker.

*obviam ivit Bruto*
The *–o* is here a closing marker referring back to *obviam ivit*.

*Bruto* **qui** *nobilis erat obviam ivit*
The **qui** is a marker of dependence (opening).

*Bruto qui nobilis* **erat** *obviam ivit*
**erat** is a closing marker of dependence.

*Bruto* **cum** *solus* **esset** *obviam ivit*
**cum** is a whole word marker (opening) of dependence.
**esset** is a whole word marker (closing) of dependence.

*Bruto* **postquam** *epistolam legit obviam ivit*
**postquam** is a whole word (opening) marker.
*–it :* inflection marker of dependence (closing) referring back to a whole word marker of dependence (opening)—*postquam.*

*Bruto* **et** *Sexto obviam ivit*
**et** *:* co-ordinating marker (between two items).

*Bruto obviam ivit* **et** *solvtavit*
**et**: co-ordinating marker between two elementary sentence blocks.

*Bruto et Sexto qui nobiles erant* **et** *qui Romam amaverunt obviam ivit* **et**: co-ordinating marker between two dependent blocks.

86

## RULES FOR STAVE ANALYSIS

1. Only the elementary sentence occupies the top stave space.

2. Dependence is shown by positioning in the stave space below.

3. All blocks in the second stave space are dependent on the elementary sentence.

4. All blocks in lower stave spaces are dependent. They depend on a block in the space above to which they are linked by one of the single vertical lines enclosing them to the right or to the left reaching up to the bottom of the space above

| | Marcus sapiens est | | |
|---|---|---|---|
| | | qui Romae habitat | |

| | Marcus | | sapiens est | |
|---|---|---|---|---|
| | | qui Romae habitat | | |

5. The opening of a block is indicated by a vertical line rising from the bottom line of the stave and cutting the stave space occupied by the block concerned to the left of the block.

6. Closing of a block is denoted by a similar line cutting the stave space to the right of the block.

7. If there are blocks dependent on this block, the vertical lines for the highest will enclose the lower blocks as well.

8. Dependent blocks, however, always have their own closures separately indicated.

9. Unrelated blocks equivalent in hierarchical status may occupy the same stave space.

| | dux cognovit | | | |
|---|---|---|---|---|
| | captivis interrogatis | | quo in loco hostes essent | |

10. They will be shown to be unrelated by a division consisting of two vertical lines between them cutting the space.

11. One of these indicates the closing of the block to the left, the other indicates the opening of the block to the right.

12. Where a part of a higher-order block is contained within a dependent block, it is isolated on the stave simply by removal to the stave space where it belongs and an appropriate gap left beneath it. No lines are necessary since they indicate dependence or closure. Neither dependence nor closure applies.

13. Two blocks juxtaposed can be separated:
   *a.* either by a double division to the top of the stave space (9)
   *b.* or a single division to the bottom of the stave space and the placing of one block on the stave below (4)
   *c.* no division but placing of one element in the space above (12)

   (a) indicates equivalence; (b) indicates dependence; (c) indicates reference upwards.

14. More than two divisions may appear side by side without intervening words, but not more than two of the same height in any grouping of vertical lines.

Multiple divisions may occur where one word is the closing word to a number of blocks, or the opening word of a number of blocks, or where two such words occur side by side.

15. If a block is separated from a block adjacent to it by two divisions of different height and a space shift, the dependence indicated by the space shift is denied by the use of the higher-reaching division.

16. Such a situation, therefore, must indicate a dependence relation with a block situated at the other end of, and above, the dependent block concerned. Hence

| | rati | | effusi | |
|---|---|---|---|---|
| | | recessisse hostes | | |

is an impossibility. Logically we can have:

| A | B | | C | |
|---|---|---|---|---|
| | rati | | effusi | |
| | | recessisse hostes | | |

B dependent on A

| | rati | | effusi | |
|---|---|---|---|---|
| | | recessisse hostes | | |

B dependent on C

| | rati | recessisse hostes | effusi | |
|---|---|---|---|---|
| | | | | |

B equivalent to A and C

89

Meaning would reveal which of the three possibilities was possible in this case, the first alternative:

... thinking that the enemy had withdrawn in disorderly array ...

## Appendix 3

# STAVE PRESENTATION OF TEXTUAL EXAMPLES

| p.11 | Marcus amicum | | | videt | |
|---|---|---|---|---|---|
| | | suum | Romae | | |
| | | | | | |
| | | | | | |

| p. 18 | | amicus sapiens est | | |
|---|---|---|---|---|
| | Meus | | | |
| | | | | |
| | | | | |

| p. 26 | Marcus | | Sextum | | videt | |
|---|---|---|---|---|---|---|
| | | magistri filius | | malum | | |
| | | | | | | |
| | | | | | | |

| p. 27 | Hic Marcus est | | |
|---|---|---|---|
| | | qui Romae habitat | |
| | | | |
| | | | |

| p. 28 | Marcus | | sapiens est | |
|---|---|---|---|---|
| | | qui Romae habitat | | |
| | | | | |
| | | | | |

| p. 28 | Marcus | | venit | | |  |
|---|---|---|---|---|---|---|
| | | ad forum | | ut panem emat | |  |
| | | | | | |  |
| | | | | | |  |

| p. 29 | captivi | | | | oraverunt |  |
|---|---|---|---|---|---|---|
| | | ut sibi parceretur | statim | | |  |
| | | | | | |  |
| | | | | | |  |

| p. 37 | ad forum | | | iit | |
|---|---|---|---|---|---|
| | | ut panem emeret | | | |
| | | | | | |
| | | | | | |

| p. 38 | | | mortuus est | | |
|---|---|---|---|---|---|
| | cum ad urbem venisset | | | | |
| | | | | | |
| | | | | | |

| p. 38 | urbem | | incenderunt | | |
|---|---|---|---|---|---|
| | | ut hostes delerent | | | |
| | | | | | |
| | | | | | |

| p. 39 | Marcum | | necavit | | |
|---|---|---|---|---|---|
| | | lapide | | | |
| | | | | | |
| | | | | | |

| p. 39 | Cum | | ex castris iisset | | |
|---|---|---|---|---|---|
| | | custodibus positis | | | |
| | | | | | |
| | | | | | |

| p. 42 | | | | satellites correptum | | traxerunt |
|---|---|---|---|---|---|---|
| Evadentem | | atque effugientem | regii | | ad regem | |
| | per forum | | | | | |

| p. 46 | | | | expedivit se exercitus |
|---|---|---|---|---|
| Hic | | | moratus | |
| | in | montibus | | |
| | propinquis urbi | | | |

| p. 79 | | cives necaverunt | |
|---|---|---|---|
| urbe capta | | | |
| | | | |
| | | | |

93

*Appendix* 4

# EXAMPLES OF SENTENCES SUBJECTED TO STAVE ANALYSIS

The two sheets of sentences that follow show in action the rules for stave analysis presented in Appendix 2. The sentences analysed were those used as a test battery for fourth and fifth form samples in the experiment referred to in the main text. The aim, during this experiment, was to stress, by the use of a five line four space stave, the *totality* of elementary sentence blocks and also of dependent blocks, and to show how a combination of these elementary sentence and dependent blocks gave to each sentence a peculiar structural hierarchy.

It was stressed in Chapter Four that it is possible to use a more sophisticated and detailed analysis by designing a stave with more lines and, consequently, more spaces. By this method it is possible to analyse any complex sentence so that Harris's strings are revealed.

The current presentation of sentences on the sheets shows both the block totality and, in some sentences, a more detailed analysis, but always on a five line, four space stave. Thus the format is somewhere between the simplest 'total block presentation' used in the research, and the most detailed analysis breaking down each sentence into units which can be strictly defined as strings. Teachers who use the method must ask themselves to what lengths they wish to go in any analysis; whether, for example, they wish to present *novarum rerum expectatione suspensos* as:

| | | | | suspensos | |
|---|---|---|---|---|---|
| | | | expectatione | | |
| | | rerum | | | |
| | novarum | | | | |

using the strictest possible analysis, or as:

| | | suspensos | |
|---|---|---|---|
| | novarum rerum expectatione | | |
| | | | |

Teachers must also decide other issues: for example, whether, in the initial stages of teaching by stave analysis, they wish to highlight the whole of both opening and closing markers in dependent units, as in:

ut per exploratores **cognosceret**

or whether to present a more strict interpretation of markers of dependence as in:

**ut** per exploratores cognosceret

Decisions of this nature may well be influenced by the degree of detail in the analysis, the level at which stave analysis is introduced etc.

| p. 28 | Marcus | | venit | | | |
|---|---|---|---|---|---|---|
| | | ad forum | | ut panem emat | | |
| | | | | | | |
| | | | | | | |

| p. 29 | captivi | | | | oraverunt | |
|---|---|---|---|---|---|---|
| | | ut sibi parceretur | statim | | | |
| | | | | | | |
| | | | | | | |

| p. 37 | ad forum | | iit | |
|---|---|---|---|---|
| | | ut panem emeret | | |
| | | | | |
| | | | | |

| p. 38 | | mortuus est | |
|---|---|---|---|
| | cum ad urbem venisset | | |
| | | | |
| | | | |

| p. 38 | urbem | | incenderunt | |
|---|---|---|---|
| | | ut hostes delerent | | |
| | | | | |
| | | | | |

| p. 39 | Marcum | | necavit | |
|---|---|---|---|
| | | lapide | | |
| | | | | |
| | | | | |

| p. 39 | Cum | | ex castris iisset | |
|---|---|---|---|
| | | custodibus positis | | |
| | | | | |
| | | | | |

## *Appendix* 3

# STAVE PRESENTATION OF TEXTUAL EXAMPLES

| p.11 | Marcus amicum | | | videt | |
|---|---|---|---|---|---|
| | | suum | Romae | | |
| | | | | | |
| | | | | | |

| p. 18. | | amicus sapiens est | |
|---|---|---|---|
| | Meus | | |
| | | | |
| | | | |

| p. 26 | Marcus | | Sextum | | videt | |
|---|---|---|---|---|---|---|
| | | magistri filius | | malum | | |
| | | | | | | |
| | | | | | | |

| p. 27 | Hic Marcus est | | |
|---|---|---|---|
| | | qui Romae habitat | |
| | | | |
| | | | |

| p. 28 | Marcus | | sapiens est | |
|---|---|---|---|
| | | qui Romae habitat | |
| | | | |
| | | | |

91

p. 42

|  |  |  |  | satellites correptum |  | traxerunt |
|---|---|---|---|---|---|---|
| Evadentem |  | atque effugientem | regii |  | ad regem |  |
|  | per forum |  |  |  |  |  |

p. 46

|  |  |  |  | expedivit se exercitus |
|---|---|---|---|---|
| Hic |  |  | moratus |  |
|  | in |  | montibus |  |
|  |  | propinquis urbi |  |  |

p. 79

|  | cives necaverunt |  |
|---|---|---|
| urbe capta |  |  |
|  |  |  |
|  |  |  |

93

## *Appendix* 4

# EXAMPLES OF SENTENCES SUBJECTED TO STAVE ANALYSIS

The two sheets of sentences that follow show in action the rules for stave analysis presented in Appendix 2. The sentences analysed were those used as a test battery for fourth and fifth form samples in the experiment referred to in the main text. The aim, during this experiment, was to stress, by the use of a five line four space stave, the *totality* of elementary sentence blocks and also of dependent blocks, and to show how a combination of these elementary sentence and dependent blocks gave to each sentence a peculiar structural hierarchy.

It was stressed in Chapter Four that it is possible to use a more sophisticated and detailed analysis by designing a stave with more lines and, consequently, more spaces. By this method it is possible to analyse any complex sentence so that Harris's strings are revealed.

The current presentation of sentences on the sheets shows both the block totality and, in some sentences, a more detailed analysis, but always on a five line, four space stave. Thus the format is somewhere between the simplest 'total block presentation' used in the research, and the most detailed analysis breaking down each sentence into units which can be strictly defined as strings. Teachers who use the method must ask themselves to what lengths they wish to go in any analysis; whether, for example, they wish to present *novarum rerum expectatione suspensos* as:

94

| | | | | suspensos | |
|---|---|---|---|---|---|
| | | | expectatione | | |
| | | rerum | | | |
| | novarum | | | | |

using the strictest possible analysis, or as:

| | | suspensos | |
|---|---|---|---|
| | novarum rerum expectatione | | |
| | | | |

Teachers must also decide other issues: for example, whether, in the initial stages of teaching by stave analysis, they wish to highlight the whole of both opening and closing markers in dependent units, as in:

ut per exploratores **cognosceret**

or whether to present a more strict interpretation of markers of dependence as in:

ut per exploratores co**gnosceret**

Decisions of this nature may well be influenced by the degree of detail in the analysis, the level at which stave analysis is introduced etc.